Teaching Well with Adolescent Learners

This concise and accessible book, co-published with the Association for Middle Level Education (AMLE), offers pre-service and in-service middle and high school educators a way to integrate an understanding of adolescent development with strong pedagogical applications for their students.

Blending contemporary research on adolescent development with authentic teachers' voices, the authors demonstrate methods for how to successfully observe, understand, engage, and teach adolescent students, particularly around the developmental changes that occur from ages 11 to 15 (grades six through ten). The book features real-world classroom narratives that illustrate the successes—and struggles—of everyday teachers, and details specific teaching practices, classroom activities, and lesson ideas that help teachers tap into the energy and talents that adolescent students bring to the classroom.

Featuring narrative case studies from teachers in the field, this practical book will be of value to middle and high school educators looking at how the physical and emotional changes experienced by students during adolescence impact their learning. It will also support scholars, practitioners, and students more broadly involved with adolescent development, classroom practice, secondary learning, and equity and inclusion in the classroom.

David Strahan is Distinguished Professor of Middle Grades Education, Emeritus, at Western Carolina University, USA.

Jeanneine Jones is Distinguished Professor of Middle Grades and Secondary Education, Emeritus, at the University of North Carolina, Charlotte, USA.

Madison White is a secondary English teacher in the Rowan Salisbury School system in North Carolina, USA.

Also Available from AMLE and Routledge
(www.routledge.com/education)

The Flexible SEL Classroom: Practical Ways to Build Social-Emotional Learning
2nd edition
Amber Chandler

Our Diverse Middle School Students: A Guide to Equitable and Responsive Teaching
Elizabeth D. Dore & Deborah H. McMurtrie

Content Area Literacy Strategies That Work: Do This, Not That!
Lori G. Wilfong

The Flexible SEL Classroom: Practical Ways to Build Social-Emotional Learning in Grades 4–8
1st edition
Amber Chandler

AMLE Innovations in Middle Level Education Research (series)
Series editor: David C. Virtue

Teaching Well with Adolescent Learners

Responding to Developmental Changes in Middle School and High School

David Strahan, Jeanneine Jones, and Madison White

Routledge
Taylor & Francis Group
NEW YORK AND LONDON

AMLE

Cover image: © Getty Images

First published 2023
by Routledge
605 Third Avenue, New York, NY 10158

and by Routledge
4 Park Square, Milton Park, Abingdon, Oxon, OX14 4RN

Routledge is an imprint of the Taylor & Francis Group, an informa business

© 2023 The Association for Middle Level Education

The right of David Strahan, Jeanneine Jones, and Madison White to be identified as authors of this work has been asserted in accordance with sections 77 and 78 of the Copyright, Designs and Patents Act 1988.

All rights reserved. No part of this book may be reprinted or reproduced or utilised in any form or by any electronic, mechanical, or other means, now known or hereafter invented, including photocopying and recording, or in any information storage or retrieval system, without permission in writing from the publishers.

Trademark notice: Product or corporate names may be trademarks or registered trademarks, and are used only for identification and explanation without intent to infringe.

Library of Congress Cataloging-in-Publication Data
Names: Strahan, David B., author. | Jones, Jeanneine P., author. | White, Madison (English teacher), author.
Title: Teaching well with adolescent learners : responding to developmental changes in middle school and high school / David Strahan, Jeanneine Jones, and Madison White.
Description: New York, NY : Routledge, 2022. | Includes bibliographical references and index.
Identifiers: LCCN 2022011204 | ISBN 9781032283890 (hardback) | ISBN 9781032283883 (paperback) | ISBN 9781003296614 (ebook)
Subjects: LCSH: Middle school teaching—United States. | High school teaching—United States. | Learning, Psychology of. | Adolescent psychology—United States.
Classification: LCC LB1623.5 .S87 2022 | DDC 373.236—dc23/eng/20220609
LC record available at https://lccn.loc.gov/2022011204

ISBN: 978-1-032-28389-0 (hbk)
ISBN: 978-1-032-28388-3 (pbk)
ISBN: 978-1-003-29661-4 (ebk)

DOI: 10.4324/9781003296614

Typeset in Palatino
by codeMantra

Still, as the spiral grew,
He left the past year's dwelling for the new,
Stole with soft step its shining archway through,
Built up its idle door,
Stretched in his last-found home, and knew the old no more

From *The Chambered Nautilus*[1]
       —By Oliver Wendell Holmes Sr.

---

[1] www.public-domain-poetry.com/oliver-wendell-holmes/chambered-nautilus-20013

Contents

List of Figures . . . . *xi*
List of Tables . . . . *xiii*
Preface . . . . *xv*
Acknowledgments . . . . *xix*

**1 Possibilities for Teaching Well with
Adolescent Learners. 1**
Teaching in Synch with Adolescent Development 3
An All-Too-Familiar Story of Beginning Teaching 6
*How Might We Better Understand the Dynamics of Teaching
   Well with Adolescent Learners?* 8
   Research on Successful Teaching 9
   Research on Adolescent Development 11
   Supportive Relationships as the Essence of
      Strong Connections 20
   Understanding and Responding to Developmental
      Changes. 22
*Classroom Narrative: Digging Deeper than the Surface Is
   Always Worth It by Madison White* 23
A Framework for Teaching Well with Adolescent Learners 26
Activities for Understanding Students Better 28
References 34
For Additional Information. 35

**2 Growing and Changing: Patterns of Physical and
Sexual Development** **38**
Understanding the Changes That Occur during Puberty 43
   Hormonal Changes 44
   Physical Changes. 45
   Pubertal Maturation. 46
Classroom Narrative: Kayla's Story by Jaleisha Hargett 48
Adultification of Students of Color 50
Recognizing Fluctuations in Energy Level and Appetite 51

Changes in Nutrition... 52
Changes in Sleep Patterns..................................... 56
Changes in Relationship to Physical Surroundings 58
Creating Classroom Communities That Nurture
  Trust and Collaboration 61
Activities for Understanding Students Better 62
References 65
For Additional Information................................... 66

3 Thinking and Feeling: Patterns of Intellectual and Emotional Development............................67
Brain Growth during Adolescence 69
Learning to Think and Feel in New Ways....................... 71
Risk, Reward, and Creativity 72
Abstract Reasoning 78
Expanding Powers of Reasoning in Lessons..................... 81
Classroom Narrative: Analysis of a Science Unit by
  Amanda Clapp.. 89
Connecting Thoughts and Feelings............................. 94
Conclusions... 102
Activities for Understanding Students Better 102
References 106

4 Reflecting and Identifying: Patterns of Personal Development..108
Developing a More Resilient Sense of Self 111
General Patterns of Identity Development 114
  Identity Development as a Negotiated Process............... 118
Figurative Transformation Activity 121
  Negotiating Ethnic-Racial and Gender Identity 123
Classroom Narrative: Supporting Charlotte and Her Classmates ... 130
Conclusions... 133
Activities for Understanding Students Better 134
Appendix: Personal Values Card Sort 137
References 147

5 Relating and Persevering: Patterns of Social and Moral Development 149

Gaining Social and Academic Competence 150
    Social Competence 150
    Academic Competence 153
Classroom Narrative: Encouraging Competency—Anthony's Case by Amie Broyhill 157
    A Small Steps Approach to Social and Academic Competence 159
Expanding Perspectives and Promoting Ethics 161
Conclusions 168
Activities for Understanding Students Better 170
References 174

6 Collaborating and Advocating: Supporting Teachers and Adolescents in Challenging Times 176

Understanding and Supporting Developmental Changes 178
    Patterns of Physical and Sexual Development 178
    Patterns of Intellectual and Emotional Development 179
    Development of Personal Identity 181
    Patterns of Social and Moral Development 182
Creating Positive Relationships 183
Implementing Responsive Teaching Practices 184
Assuring the Necessary Conditions for a Threshold of Engagement: Classroom Communities That Nurture Trust and Collaboration 185
Understanding Challenges to Positive Youth Development 186
The Story of Ms. Hutchison Revisited 192
References 203

Index 205

Figures

1.1	"Crowned with color," self-portrait by Izzy S.	4
1.2	Reading and growing with opportunities	19
1.3	A framework for teaching well with adolescent learners	27
2.1	Youthful perspectives	44
2.2	Shared selfies	53
3.1	Modeling to enhance representational thinking	79
3.2	"My soccer goals," digital art by Ellie C.	96
3.3	Gabrielle's concept map of concepts related to density (student artwork)	103
4.1	"I am poem" by Faye A.	113
5.1	Celebrating teamwork	152
5.2	Mature perspective-taking	163
6.1	A framework for teaching well with adolescent learners	177
6.2	Gaining confidence	184
6.3	Teaching well with a spirit of adventure	190

Tables

1.1	Search Institute's Framework of Developmental Assets	14
3.1	My Decision-Making Plan	77
3.2	Responses of Sixth Graders to a Reading and Thinking Problem	80
3.3	Levels of Understanding in a Progression from Surface to Deep	84
6.1	Teaching Well with Adolescent Learners: Connections with *The Successful Middle School: This We Believe*	191

Preface

School is a unique place and no one understands it quite like those who teach and learn there. The three of us have spent our professional lives in schools. Early in our careers, we became intrigued with the vitality and strength of the adolescents whose energy filled the hallways of middle and high schools. We were inspired by the teachers who appreciated and nurtured them. We were blessed with mentors who believed in us and who shared their wisdom of practice with us. Once we gained teaching confidence in our own classrooms, we learned the joys of observing the lessons of other teachers and we added research to the skills we valued. As students of teaching, we have now accumulated a wealth of information and insight, and we have shared some of this wisdom in the pages of this text.

Little did we know how timely our labors would become when we began our work. We have heard a great deal about heroes over the past couple of years as the pandemic rages around the world, and, in this unprecedented time, we are reminded of a declaration from Christopher Reeve: "A hero is an ordinary individual who finds the strength to persevere and endure in spite of overwhelming obstacles." We have indeed witnessed many obstacles—and heroes—in the hallways of schools and in their virtual classrooms; here teachers grapple with students' developmental needs and pandemic fears while still expecting the rigor required for solid content learning.

As we move to final production of our text, the pandemic continues to threaten the health and wellness of students and teachers. Life in classrooms is stressful and, in some cases, contentious. Youth have been especially vulnerable to the risks that attack their mental health, and these urgent concerns, among many others, have been widely expressed in the media:

- Once-normal aspects of school life—lunchtime, extracurricular activities, assemblies, school trips, parent-teacher conferences, reliable bus schedules—have been eliminated or have become unpredictable.
- Many children and teenagers are experiencing mental health problems. Isolation and disruption are taking a serious toll on their emotional and social development. Many students are reporting a sense of apathy and hopelessness.
- Suicide attempts have risen. Emergency room personnel report dramatic increases in cases and support services are often understaffed.
- Gun violence against children has increased, as has a broader nationwide rise in crime.
- Indicators of academic achievement show serious declines, with the most vulnerable youth falling further behind their classmates.

Alongside these troubling headlines, we have experienced heated disagreements about face-to-face instruction, the effectiveness of virtual teaching and learning, and mask mandates. Beneath the angry voices, however, a realization has been tested and solidified: Schools are absolutely essential to the healthy development of children. With that expectation front and center, teachers feel even more overwhelmed as they work to connect with their students and to enhance their resiliency and personal identity.

In these exceptional times, the essential conditions for good education are more important than ever. Teenagers need teachers who care for them authentically. They need adults who listen and understand. They need spaces where they are valued, where they belong and feel safe. They need lessons that engage their senses, challenge them to think deeply, and prepare them for their successful place in an uncertain world.

We examine many of these essential conditions in this book, and especially the ways teachers can come to understand better their adolescent students, in turn creating classrooms grounded in authentic caring. With a flourishing cadre of advocates for positive youth development, we are optimistic about increased opportunities for stronger systems of protection and challenge that inspire our teen students. We trust that *Teaching Well with Adolescent Learners* will be an additional vehicle for advocacy as it helps guide efforts that enhance the well-being of youth.

In closing, we dedicate our book to the many hundreds of great teachers we have known, and we hope you will recognize yourselves in these pages; you have taught us well. Thank you for everything you have given so selflessly to your students—and us. We look forward to your continuing inspiration and to the myriad possibilities your students find in your care. We hope we have done your good work justice.

David Strahan

Jeanneine Jones

Madison White
February 2, 2022

Acknowledgments

We would like to thank the colleagues who contributed so generously to our book.

Jaleisha Hargett, Amanda Clapp, and Amie Broyhill shared their classroom narratives with us and gave us permission to print them. Their first-hand accounts document ways good teachers understand and respond to students. These narratives helped bring our book to life.

Janine Campbell from Byron Center West Middle School in Byron Center, Michigan helped us identify student artwork to illustrate our themes. Her students, Izzie and Ellie, gave us two great examples and granted us permission to publish them. We thank the three of them.

Stephanie Simpson, Chief Executive Officer of the Association for Middle Level Education, encouraged us from the beginning and helped us secure permission to print the "I am poem" by Faye A which encapsulates, with student voice, many key points this book expresses.

Hundreds of others, far too many teachers to name, inspired us with their energy and commitment to adolescents. We hope our book helps advance their mission.

1

Possibilities for Teaching Well with Adolescent Learners

> When I am teaching a lesson, I watch students' eyes to see if the picture is growing clear. When I see those pictures in their eyes, that is the "aha" moment for me. If I see the pictures begin to fade, I know I have to adjust the lesson to bring the pictures back. That's the excitement that keeps me going.

Successful teachers are great observers of their students. As noted in her quotation above, a friend once described ways that she watched for "pictures" to form in the minds of her students. Those moments when she could see them forming were energizing for her. Knowing how to see pictures form and how to keep them developing is a great metaphor for joy in teaching. This heightened responsiveness is especially important when teaching students in middle and high school. At this time of life, children are becoming adolescents. Bodies are changing. Thoughts are growing more sophisticated, peer dynamics more complicated.

As teachers and teacher observers, Jeanneine and Dave have spent more than 80 years in middle and high school classrooms. We began this book as a way to share some of the inspiration and mystery of teaching that keep us working well past the age when we might have retired. To add a fresh perspective, we invited Madison to join us as a third author. As an early career teacher, she is finding how the excitement of engaging lessons becomes addictive. She is also immersed in the day-to-day challenges of teaching high school students, some of whom have a history of frustration with schooling. The three of us are committed to providing the best possible educational experiences for students, especially those in transition from childhood to adolescence. That is why we chose the phrase "teaching well" for our title and emphasized both middle and high school.

The three of us have been fortunate to work with teachers who have inspired us with their energy, creativity, and commitment. Time and again, we have experienced the enthusiasm these teachers have generated. In the most animated classrooms, engagement becomes addictive for them and for their students. Unfortunately, joy in learning is not always the norm. Classrooms can be stressful environments. Sometimes students cannot wait for the day to end and, in the worst cases, neither can their teachers.

What makes the difference? We are convinced that powerful learning experiences are co-constructed. Teachers and students draw energy from each other as they explore ideas, examine problems, wrestle with concepts, or enjoy simple moments together. The essential condition for these experiences is that students and teachers understand each other. Understanding begins with the teacher. That insight is the starting place for our book: successful teachers understand and respond to adolescent learners, as groups and as individuals. Understanding adolescents better enables teachers to establish stronger working relationships with them as individuals, create deeper academic connections with them, and draw energy from them as they develop their strengths in the classroom.

Appreciating changes, tapping students' energy, and creating connections are the primary goals of this book. Our basic premise is straightforward: the better we understand our students, the better we can create caring connections with them, connections that draw them into learning as partners in the process. From this perspective, teaching well begins with understanding and supporting developmental changes.

In this book, we examine the changes that occur from ages 11 to 15. This time span encompasses the onset of puberty, a cultural milestone that marks the end of childhood. It includes the experiences that precede eligibility for a driver's license and permits to work part-time, cultural milestones that mark the beginning of adolescence. The differences between sixth graders and high school students are dramatic, and the developmental changes that occur during these years are unique in the lifespan. In the rest of this chapter, we will describe how good teachers find ways to tap the energy and talents students bring to the classroom. Instead of regarding developmental changes as obstacles to overcome, they teach in synch with adolescent development.

Teaching in Synch with Adolescent Development

We trust that the reviews of research and classroom stories we share in this text will help readers better understand their students as both groups and individuals. We anticipate that this information will be especially useful to pre-service teachers preparing to teach and to beginning teachers entering the profession from all pathways. Veteran teachers will likely find that the research shared here provides affirmation or new insights into their teaching, and the candid teacher stories of successes and stumbles may even mirror their own. When contemplated from the viewpoint of full school faculty or university program study, these dynamics provide a strong platform for engaging discussion, broadened perspectives, and solid mentoring.

We are especially grateful to the Association for Middle Level Education (AMLE) for encouraging us to write this text and supporting the transition from manuscript to finished product. AMLE has been our professional home for four decades. The most recent version of the association's foundational position paper, *The Successful Middle School: This We Believe* (2021) by Penny Bishop and Lisa Harrison, has been our guiding beacon as we completed the manuscript. As they emphasize, being responsive to the needs of adolescents has been "the hallmark of middle level education since the field's inception" (p. 55).

> The middle school years are an exciting time, as young adolescents are in the midst of profound personal change and identity development. They are growing physically,

intellectually, morally, psychologically, and socio-emotionally. They are thinking deeply about who they are in relation to their race, ethnicity, social class, gender, sexual orientation, religion, and other identities. They are beginning to ponder some of the quintessential questions of life.

(p. 3)

The Successful Middle School presents, in detail, the conditions necessary to support and guide our young people through these changes. The authors describe evidence-based practices that are responsive, challenging, empowering, equitable, and engaging. Providing those practices for all students during the transition from childhood to early adulthood is the central mission of AMLE.

As we examine these dynamics of transition, we emphasize a positive perspective on youth development and teaching. Public perceptions of schooling that spans the transition from the later elementary years to the final years of high school are

Figure 1.1 "Crowned with color," self-portrait by Izzy S.

often stereotyped. Students are difficult to teach. Classrooms are rowdy. Parents become discouraged. As our book unfolds, we acknowledge the genuine challenges of teaching and learning during this developmental time span. We show how successful teachers address difficult obstacles. Each chapter features real-world narratives written by teachers we know well, reports that capture their frustrations as well as their successes. Chapters also feature sections entitled "activities for understanding students better" that offer concrete, specific strategies for learning more about students and generating engagement.

In summary, this book is about understanding our adolescent students. Although we offer good examples of successful practices, it is not a book about classroom management or teaching content, for we have learned that understanding our students first makes these other things possible.

Beginning teachers and sometimes those with years of experience can feel overwhelmed.

Classrooms are complex systems that are difficult to predict. There are so many different personalities, abrupt changes by the minute, actions and reactions far different from what we anticipated the day before as we head-rehearsed the lesson. There are behaviors to consider and differentiation to plan—there is so much to account for that it is impossible to identify a set of practices that works all the time for everyone, or even at different times for the same person. And yet, we have to figure out how to survive and thrive, and we must do so in the moment.

Step 1 is getting to know our students well. Only then can we break down those complexities, better anticipate the changes, and more accurately predict classroom dynamics.

With all this in mind, consider these suggestions as you read this book:

- When you read our research reports, ask yourself, "How does this connect with my students?"
- When you read our classroom examples and teachers' stories, ask yourself, "How does this relate to my experience?"
- When you find yourself wanting to know more or wondering how to put our suggestions into practice, ask

yourself, "Where can I go to get more good information quickly?" For example, the website for the Association for Middle Level Education is one of our primary resources. There you can search for your topic and find articles or podcasts that give concrete, specific up-to-date ideas. (https://www.amle.org/). Another suggestion might be your content area's professional association, where you also will find many helpful resources like journal articles, blogs, and engaging methodologies for teaching your subject.

An All-Too-Familiar Story of Beginning Teaching

To illustrate the importance of teaching in synch with adolescent development, we begin with the story of Ms. Hutchinson, a hypothetical composite of several teachers we have known well. Ms. Hutchinson graduated from her university with a degree in Environmental Studies and a passion for science. During her final semester, she was recruited to join a research team that gathered information about plant growth in Costa Rica. In this project, Ms. Hutchinson put her scientific training into action and began taking graduate courses. She loved the work, but she missed her family and friends in North Carolina. She learned of a Master's in a teaching program, which would enable her to begin teaching while learning on the job. She decided to give teaching a try. She began courses in a summer session and enjoyed the training seminars that provided basic information about curriculum, lesson plans, assessment, and classroom management.

When the school year started, she quickly embraced her new routine. She immersed herself in the ninth-grade science content, met with colleagues to learn school procedures, talked to fellow science teachers to discuss curriculum expectations, and arranged an inviting classroom with photos of Costa Rica and an aquarium. During the first weeks of school, she worked hard to learn students' names, encouraged them to be respectful of each other, and planned science experiments to motivate them to think like scientists.

She was surprised when many of her students did not engage with the experiments. In class discussions, few responded to questions, and those who did so often seemed confused about basic scientific concepts. Many participated superficially, distracted with their cellular devices and sometimes putting their heads on their desks and pretending to sleep. Occasionally, arguments between students flared loudly. When she asked a few of her fellow teachers for advice, they did not provide much help. Some were new to the profession, as she was. Others emphasized getting tougher: assign more seat work to focus on discipline, offer harsher penalties, and send students to the office.

By the end of the first semester, Ms. Hutchinson was not sure she could make it as a teacher. The university courses she was taking were intellectually interesting with stimulating discussions, yet not very helpful in addressing her immediate challenges. Before and after class she talked at length with some of her fellow students and found that they, too, felt as though they were drowning in their classrooms. Like her, they struggled to find ways to reach their students and most strategies didn't seem particularly effective. Over the holidays, Ms. Hutchison sent an email to her former supervisor asking about possibilities for other research grant work. She hoped she might have another position by summer.

Before we continue Ms. Hutchinson's story, let us consider some of the challenges she was facing. Many of these had become her daily litany:

- ♦ My students are generally nice kids, but they don't care about school.
- ♦ They haven't had enough science to understand what I'm teaching.
- ♦ My older colleagues don't really see the big picture and aren't doing much better than I am.
- ♦ This school system doesn't provide enough support for beginning teachers.
- ♦ My university courses are interesting, but they don't help me with the day-to-day realities of my classroom.

Ms. Hutchinson could probably add to this list, but we think it is important to consider some of the other challenges she faced, challenges of which she may not have been fully aware:

- ♦ Ms. Hutchinson loves science. Thinking science has become second nature to her.
- ♦ Her understanding of science has become automatic to the extent that it is almost impossible for her to pinpoint the details that constitute ideas. This makes it difficult for her to grasp why students do not always understand her lessons.
- ♦ Ms. Hutchinson has not been a ninth grader for at least ten years. She thinks like an adult and can no longer think like an adolescent. Even if she could, the world of her students is very different—in both time and setting—from her experiences when she was that age.

In other words, Ms. Hutchinson's knowledge of science and her perspective as an adult limits her comprehension of students' thoughts and feelings. To understand how her students view themselves and their approaches to science content, she needs to develop new ways of thinking.

How Might We Better Understand the Dynamics of Teaching Well with Adolescent Learners?

Fortunately for Ms. Hutchinson and others like her, the story does not have to end in frustration or career change. When we continue her story in our final chapter, we will describe how her administrator recognized her doubts and opened doors for a mindset shift. Further, we will detail how her colleagues helped her better understand her students through perceptive advice and practical mentoring. This change in mindset guided her back into her university coursework with a more confident voice and an enlightened insight. All this, in turn, led her to embrace the profession that she once thought had defeated her.

In the rest of this chapter, we will introduce these foundational ways of thinking. We will then describe two essential conditions for improving practice: developing supportive relationships with students and learning to understand them better—as groups and as individuals.

Research on Successful Teaching

In time, Ms. Hutchinson learned to appreciate the energy adolescents bring to learning tasks and to design her lessons with them in mind. She did so with encouragement and guidance from colleagues who had learned to draw strength and insight from two intertwined sources of information: research on successful teaching and research on adolescent development.

Our own careers have provided opportunities for participation in a number of strong research projects examining successful teaching at the middle and high school levels. In this section, we summarize insights from those sources we have found most informative in our own work, both the research we have generated and those studies from which we have learned. (For an illustrative listing of research reports from our projects, see the For Additional Information section in the References).

These research projects have provided rich descriptions of practices that teachers have developed collaboratively. Successful teachers develop a wisdom of practice. They share insights with colleagues and reflect thoughtfully about their own learning. In his classic studies of reflective practice, Schon (1983) characterized these connected ways of knowing as reflection in action and reflection on action. Since then, thousands of studies have generated a wealth of information about good teaching and ways good teachers get better.

To illustrate one small strand of this research, we will summarize a report published in Roney and Lipka's (2013) *Middle Grades Curriculum: Voices and Visions of the Self-Enhancing School*. In a chapter entitled "Understanding Learners: From Confusion About Learners to Clear Understanding of Learner Characteristics," Strahan (2013) analyzed a series of six case studies with successful teachers. These studies featured intensive qualitative research that tapped the wisdom of practice of participants

(Strahan, Smith, McElrath, & Toole, 2001; Smith & Strahan, 2004; Strahan & Layell, 2006; Strahan, Faircloth, Cope, & Hundley, 2007; Kronenberg and Strahan, 2010; Binkley, Keiser, & Strahan, 2011). When considered together, these six studies documented four recurring patterns of success:

- These good teachers addressed students' basic needs for physical and emotional safety. They created classroom communities that nurtured trusting relationships. They built trust with students in conversations that helped them learn more about students as individuals. They also promoted positive relationships among students so that they could support each other.
- These good teachers planned instructional activities that responded to students' academic needs and interests. They developed assignments that linked inquiry and collaboration. These assignments provided rich data for assessing students' progress in learning strategies and concepts. Participants integrated content and procedures to foster a sense of "connectedness." They focused attention on social and ethical dimensions of learning by extending the community beyond the walls of their classrooms. Family and community activities provided opportunities for real-world experiences.
- These good teachers provided ongoing personal support to students. They not only described in detail the emotional, physical, intellectual and family needs and circumstances of students but also addressed these needs by responding to students as individuals.
- These good teachers engaged students in dialogue that helped them make personal connections with their classroom experiences. They encouraged students to reflect on how they learned as well as what they learned. They nurtured intrinsic motivation by involving students in classroom decisions on a continuous basis. As students gained confidence, participants encouraged them to set goals and assume more responsibility for their learning.

(Strahan, 2013, p. 216)

In the conversations chronicled in these six studies, investigators rarely heard teachers use the language of researchers to express their understanding of their students, formal terms like "developmental needs," "physical changes," "cognitive growth," or "identity development." Rather, in day-to-day conversations, teachers often made comments like

- Students this age are so different.
- Some seventh graders look like high schoolers; others still seem so young.
- Puberty brings all sorts of changes and issues.
- Hormones kick in at awkward times.
- Middle school students think differently.
- They need to find out who they are.
- What their peers think of them is so important.
- Sometimes everything is black or white with students; they have a hard time seeing shades of gray.

(Strahan, 2013, p. 216)

These real-world comments provide glimpses of the insights that guide the decisions of successful teachers. In the chapters that follow, we will draw from both formal and informal studies of successful middle school and high school teaching to show how teachers can learn to better understand their students.

Research on Adolescent Development

Another essential source of information is the data reported in a growing number of studies on adolescent development. Researchers with different areas of expertise are exploring issues related to development: neurobiology, health, social services, counseling, and psychology, as well as curriculum, instruction, and appropriate forms of assessment. For those of us in education, it is exciting to have so much good research information available. Sometimes our challenge is making sense of it.

One important theme in recent research is a positive perspective on youth development. For much of the twentieth century, research and practice focused on deficit issues in development, often at the expense of many positive aspects. For example, the adolescent period was long plagued by themes of storm and stress, portraying adolescence as a time to be endured. Adolescence was turbulent, traumatic, and troublesome. Adolescents needed structure and control.

Unfortunately, this legacy continues to some extent. All of us who teach in middle schools or high schools have experienced a familiar scenario. When we strike up a casual conversation with someone new, and they ask what we do, we hear comments like "how can you spend your day with adolescents?" or "you must have a lot of patience," or "bless you!" Comments like these remind us that the public often stereotypes adolescents as difficult or out of control. A few comments from parents capture some of these frequent concerns:

> *I don't know what happened to her over the summer. She used to be so sweet and cooperative. Now, it seems she wants to argue with me over almost anything.*
>
> *Boy, sometimes I just don't know where he's coming from. I'm afraid he will give up his soccer dreams and disappear into a cave of loud music and video games.*
>
> *All she wants to think about is her friends—on Instagram, Snapchat, and TikTok all the time. We have a big battle every night about putting the phone away at dinnertime—let alone putting it away to do homework.*
>
> *He was doing really well with math—until he got to middle school. I don't know if it's this new curriculum or what, but his teacher says he just isn't keeping up.*

Comments like these are familiar. Students do change as they leave childhood. These changes can be bewildering. Even though we expect this, we need to know more about the unique developmental changes adolescents are experiencing if we are to nurture strong classroom connections effectively with them.

Fortunately, the science of child and adolescent development provides excellent information. One of the most helpful frameworks for understanding and responding to changes is "Developmental Assets." First designed in the 1990s and regularly updated since, the Developmental Assets framework provides a set of benchmarks for understanding and supporting positive aspects of development (Benson, Leffert, Scales, & Blyth, 1998). Researchers at the Search Institute designed the framework from empirical studies with a focus on protective factors and resiliency, as well as extensive surveys of youth perceptions. They examined the 40 assets identified in a study with more than 250,000 students. Since their original studies, the Search Institute has continued to investigate assets and strengthen its understanding of development (Search Institute, 2018a, 2018b, 2018c). In the paragraphs that follow, we summarize key findings and show how understanding assets can enhance teaching.

Assets are organized in two major domains, internal and external, which detail the strengths youth may develop within themselves (such as commitments, values, and competencies), and the supports they may possess from family and community (health-promoting features of the environment). The External Assets are grouped into four categories:

a   Support,
b   Empowerment,
c   Boundaries and Expectations, and
d   Constructive Use of Time.

The Internal Assets are placed in four categories:

a   Commitment to Learning,
b   Positive Values,
c   Social Competencies, and
d   Positive Identity.

Table 1.1 provides a complete list of the 40 assets.

The assets framework has proven highly associated with positive outcomes in health, wellness, and achievement (Scales, Benson, Leffert, & Blyth, 2000; Roehlkepartain, 2015). Adolescents who possess more assets are more likely to do well in

Table 1.1 Search Institute's Framework of Developmental Assets

40 Developmental Assets® for Adolescents (ages 12-18)

Search Institute® has identified the following building blocks of healthy development—known as Developmental Assets®—that help young people grow up healthy, caring, and responsible.

External Assets

Support

1. **Family support**—Family life provides high levels of love and support.
2. **Positive family communication**—Young person and her or his parent(s) communicate positively, and young person is willing to seek advice and counsel from parents.
3. **Other adult relationships**—Young person receives support from three or more nonparent adults.
4. **Caring neighborhood**—Young person experiences caring neighbors.
5. **Caring school climate**—School provides a caring, encouraging environment.
6. **Parent involvement in schooling**—Parent(s) are actively involved in helping young person succeed in school.

Empowerment

7. **Community values youth**—Young person perceives that adults in the community value youth.
8. **Youth as resources**—Young people are given useful roles in the community.
9. **Service to others**—Young person serves in the community one hour or more per week.
10. **Safety**—Young person feels safe at home, school, and in the neighborhood.

Boundaries & Expectations

11. **Family boundaries**—Family has clear rules and consequences and monitors the young person's whereabouts.
12. **School Boundaries**—School provides clear rules and consequences.
13. **Neighborhood boundaries**—Neighbors take responsibility for monitoring young people's behavior.
14. **Adult role models**—Parent(s) and other adults model positive, responsible behavior.
15. **Positive peer influence**—Young person's best friends model responsible behavior.
16. **High expectations**—Both parent(s) and teachers encourage the young person to do well.

Constructive Use of Time

17. **Creative activities**—Young person spends three or more hours per week in lessons or practice in music, theater, or other arts.
18. **Youth programs**—Young person spends three or more hours per week in sports, clubs, or organizations at school and/or in the community.

19. **Religious community**—Young person spends one or more hours per week in activities in a religious institution.
20. **Time at home**—Young person is out with friends "with nothing special to do" two or fewer nights per week.

Internal Assets

Commitment to Learning

21. **Achievement Motivation**—Young person is motivated to do well in school.
22. **School Engagement**—Young person is actively engaged in learning.
23. **Homework**—Young person reports doing at least one hour of homework every school day.
24. **Bonding to school**—Young person cares about her or his school.
25. **Reading for Pleasure**—Young person reads for pleasure three or more hours per week.

Positive Values

26. **Caring**—Young person places high value on helping other people.
27. **Equality and social justice**—Young person places high value on promoting equality and reducing hunger and poverty.
28. **Integrity**—Young person acts on convictions and stands up for her or his beliefs.
29. **Honesty**—Young person "tells the truth even when it is not easy."
30. **Responsibility**—Young person accepts and takes personal responsibility.
31. **Restraint**—Young person believes it is important not to be sexually active or to use alcohol or other drugs.

Social Competencies

32. **Planning and decision making**—Young person knows how to plan ahead and make choices.
33. **Interpersonal Competence**—Young person has empathy, sensitivity, and friendship skills.
34. **Cultural Competence**—Young person has knowledge of and comfort with people of different cultural/racial/ethnic backgrounds.
35. **Resistance skills**—Young person can resist negative peer pressure and dangerous situations.
36. **Peaceful conflict resolution**—Young person seeks to resolve conflict nonviolently.

Positive Identity

37. **Personal power**—Young person feels he or she has control over "things that happen to me."
38. **Self-esteem**—Young person reports having a high self-esteem.
39. **Sense of purpose**—Young person reports that "my life has a purpose."
40. **Positive view of personal future**—Young person is optimistic about her or his personal future.

This page may be reproduced for educational, noncommercial uses only. Copyright © 1997, 2006 by Search Institute, 3001 Broadway St. N.E., Suite 310, Minneapolis, MN 55413; 800-888-7828; www.searchinstitute.org. All Rights Reserved.
The following are registered trademarks of Search Institute: Search Institute®, Developmental Assets® and Healthy Communities Healthy Youth®.

school, report stronger perceptions of themselves, and avoid risky behaviors.

> Since the first study, we have consistently found that the more assets young people experience, the better off they are. Young people with more Developmental Assets report lower levels of high-risk behaviors (such as alcohol use and violence) and higher levels of thriving attitudes and behaviors (such as doing well in school, leadership, and valuing diversity). This association has been shown to be true across every population studied, from major cities in the United States to rural villages in Uganda.
> (Roehlkepartain, 2015, p. 1)

The Developmental Assets framework provides a foundation for a better understanding of the changes that occur during adolescence, and the strengths students bring with them to school. As teachers, we can readily identify the areas of asset development most closely related to day-to-day lessons. For example, we influence all of the assets within the Commitment to Learning cluster every day in our classrooms:

- Achievement motivation—Young person is motivated to do well in school.
- School engagement—Young person is actively engaged in learning.
- Homework—Young person reports doing at least one hour of homework every school day.
- Bonding to school—Young person cares about her or his school.
- Reading for pleasure—Young person reads for pleasure for three or more hours per week.

We also influence the assets identified in the framework that develop Positive Values, including Caring, Equality, Social justice, Integrity, Honesty, Responsibility, and Restraint. Our lessons can foster Social Competencies such as Planning and decision-making, Interpersonal competence, Cultural competence,

Resistance skills, and Peaceful conflict resolution. Part of our mission as teachers is to promote the assets of Positive Identity: Personal power, Self-esteem, Sense of purpose, and Positive view of personal future. From this perspective, teachers focus naturally on building assets.

The Developmental Assets framework also helps us better understand some of the differences among groups of students in their perceptions of themselves and of the support they receive. Results from surveys of more than 120,000 students in grades 6–12 showed that ratings of assets varied by demographic categories.

- In general, female respondents were more positive about three of the four Internal Assets (Commitment to Learning, Positive Values, Social Competencies).
- Males showed somewhat stronger perceptions of Positive Identity and Safety.
- In the External Assets categories, White and Multi-racial respondents reported more positive perceptions of other adult relationships than did African American, American Indian, Asian American, and Latinx American respondents (more than 10% differences). Latinx respondents were less positive about youth programs.
- In the Internal Assets categories, African American, American Indian, Asian American, and Latinx American reported lower School engagement and Peaceful conflict resolution. Asian American respondents reported higher perceptions of Restraint and lower perceptions of Self-esteem.
- When compared with non-LGBT respondents, lesbian, gay, bi-sexual, and transgender youth were less positive about three of the External Assets categories (Support, Empowerment, Boundaries and Expectations), all four aspects of Positive Identity, and 8 of the other 16 Internal Assets (Achievement motivation, School engagement, Bonding to school, Honesty, Responsibility, Restraint, Planning and decision-making, Resistance skills).

(Search Institute, 2018c)

Continuing research has expanded our understanding of the developmental changes that enhance strengths and exacerbate disparities. In 2019, the National Academies of Sciences, Engineering, and Medicine published a monumental report synthesizing this research. Entitled *The Promise of Adolescence: Realizing Opportunity for All Youth,* this report resulted from the collaboration of 18 researchers in the fields of neurobiological and socio-behavioral sciences of adolescent development. These researchers examined hundreds of recent investigations and considered ways this information might be applied to promote adolescent well-being, resilience, and development and address issues of inequality. The report features detailed analyses of pubertal, neurobiological, cognitive, and psychosocial changes occurring during adolescence. In their conclusions, the authors issue a powerful call for understanding development as a source of strength rather than deficit.

> While often thought of as a time of turmoil and risk for young people, adolescence is more accurately viewed as a developmental period rich with opportunity for youth to learn and grow. If provided with the proper support and protection, normal processes of growth and maturation can lead youth to form healthy relationships with their peers and families, develop a sense of identity and self, and experience enriching and memorable engagements with the world. Adolescence thus forms a critical bridge between childhood and adulthood and is a critical window of opportunity for positive, life-altering development. As a positive window of opportunity, adolescence marks a period of optimism, where the assets of youth and their development may be capitalized for the betterment of society.
>
> (National Academies of Sciences, Engineering, and Medicine, 2019, p. 75)

Figure 1.2 Reading and growing with opportunities

These insights from research on adolescent development provided a trove of information for us to consider as we wrote this book. As we share insights in the chapters that follow, we will try to focus on patterns of development in ways that do not limit perceptions of students or contribute to stereotypes.

For example, one powerful pattern of development is that during the time period of early adolescence, most students begin to think more abstractly. Younger students often think more concretely. The better middle and high school teachers understand these changes in thinking, the more able they are to scaffold instruction so that students can build on familiar, concrete ideas. Knowing our students better helps us also realize that there are many individual differences within general patterns. When offered an opportunity to explore an abstraction such as freedom or theme, students may express wonderful insights that demonstrate sophisticated thoughts. Successful teachers use their knowledge of general patterns of development and their understanding of individuals to create a healthy mix of familiar and new.

Supportive Relationships as the Essence of Strong Connections

Heightened awareness of developmental changes underscores the importance of supportive relationships. For many years, researchers have shown conclusively that relationships are the single most important factor in school success. In 2017, The Search Institute synthesized much of this research and integrated its findings with data from longitudinal projects involving more than 25,000 students in grades six through twelve. In a report entitled *Relationships First: Creating Connections that Help Young People Thrive*, the authors documented key factors of students' success linked with the power of their relationships with adults and peers (Roehlkepartain et al., 2017). Measures of four essential aspects of well-being were significantly higher among students who reported strong webs of relationships:

- Academic motivation—students care about how they do in school and try as hard as they can to do their best work
- Socio-Emotional skills—students recognize and respect other people's feelings and are good at making and keeping friends
- Responsibility—students take responsibility for their own actions and do their best even on tasks they don't like
- High-Risk behaviors—students are less likely to engage in high-risk behaviors, such as alcohol use, tobacco use, or violent behaviors.

(p. 9)

The magnitude of this power is dramatic. Researchers concluded:

> Middle school students who reported high levels of developmental relationships with their teachers were eight times more likely to stick with challenging tasks, enjoy working hard, and know it is okay to make mistakes when learning, when compared to students with low levels of student-teacher relationships.
>
> (p. 8)

As Peter Benson, one of the lead researchers at the Search Institute, noted,

> After decades of forming hypotheses, conducting surveys, crafting and rewriting definitions, analyzing data, and writing journal articles, Search Institute researchers and practitioners have arrived at a surprisingly simple conclusion: nothing—*nothing*—has more impact in the life of a child than positive relationships.
>
> (p. 3)

Not only did the Search Institute researchers document the importance of relationships, but they also described how developmental relationships are characterized by a dynamic mix of five essential elements:

- Expressing care—showing that students matter
- Challenging growth—pushing students to keep getting better
- Providing support—helping students complete tasks and achieve goals
- Sharing power—treating students with respect and giving them a say
- Expanding possibilities—connecting students with people and places that broaden their horizons

(p. 4)

The *Relationships First* report underscores the importance of trust in relationships among teachers and students (Roehlkepartain et al., 2017). In a now-classic investigation, Goddard, Tschannen-Moran, and Hoy (2001) examined ways that learning depends on trust. Data from 47 elementary schools showed that measures of trust consistently predicted achievement differences in mathematics and reading, even when they controlled for race, gender, socioeconomic status, and past achievement. They concluded, "When teachers believe their students are competent and reliable, they create learning environments that facilitate students' academic success. When students trust their teachers, they are more likely to take the risks that new learning entails" (p. 14). Unfortunately, when the opposite dynamics occur, a "self-reinforcing spiral of blame and suspicion" hampers student achievement (p. 15).

When considered together, these studies help us to better understand the dynamics of supportive relationships. Students who have experienced limited success in school are often caught in a vicious cycle of poor performance and limited effort. Because they have not learned as much as they might have, they have limited background knowledge to guide new academic connections and little motivation to take the risks necessary to engage with activities. Learning to trust a teacher is the only way to break this cycle. Trusting a caring teacher increases the willingness to take chances and invest effort in new challenges. Trusting relationships thus constitute a threshold of action, a point beyond which meaningful learning can occur.

When integrated with findings from research on good teaching and studies of adolescent development, these insights about the power of relationships provide a foundation for understanding the ways teachers and students might create stronger connections in varied classroom settings.

Understanding and Responding to Developmental Changes
Earlier in this chapter, we shared the story of Ms. Hutchinson, a beginning ninth-grade teacher with expertise in science and great intentions toward students. Despite her hard work and passion for her subject matter, she became so frustrated with the lack of response from students that she considered quitting the profession. In our concluding chapter, we will share the rest of the story in which Ms. Hutchinson found a supportive group of fellow teachers who helped her better understand her students, change her approach, and become a healthier, happier teacher. For now, her story illustrates the challenges—and heartaches—of teaching in ways that are not fully in harmony with adolescence.

As we have indicated, our fundamental premise is that the better we understand our students, the better we can create caring connections with them, connections that draw them into learning as partners in the process. This is what we mean by teaching in sync with adolescence. We take to heart the call from the authors of *The Promise of Adolescence: Realizing Opportunity for All Youth* to embrace adolescence as a "positive window of opportunity" (National Academies of Sciences, Engineering, and Medicine, 2019, p. 75). We will examine fundamental patterns of development and offer suggestions for tapping the strengths of students experiencing these changes. We have learned that each of these patterns of development can provide opportunities for engagement and energy. For example, students often want to spend time with peers. With the proper structure and support, group work during lessons can be an opportunity for both socialization and collaborative learning. Not only do students experience and strengthen social relationships, but they also think together about ideas that strengthen their academic understanding.

To provide a concrete, specific example of ways teachers create caring connections with students by teaching in sync with their development, we share the first of our narratives from teachers.

> **Classroom Narrative: Digging Deeper than the Surface Is Always Worth It**
>
> By Madison White, South Rowan High School, China Grove, NC
>
> There are always students in the building known only too well by every teacher in every department across the entire school, whether by name or experience. Their reputations roll before them like a loud wave, be that for positive accolades and good citizenship or for office referrals and disruptive behaviors. No matter how early on you are in your career, you expect them—there are always those students you just know before you ever really *know* them.
>
> Jameson was a perfect example of being known for that latter reputation—he was a fighter with a record full of suspensions, foul language, and poor academic efforts. Teachers would freely share how they couldn't imagine trying to manage a classroom that included Jameson on a daily basis, and most of those teachers had never even met him.
>
> And me? Oh, I was as guilty as anyone for questioning my ability to teach this young man, let alone manage his reputed bad behavior. When I received my rosters and skimmed the one for my yearlong English 1 class, the first name I noticed was Jameson's and my stomach dropped. I was a second-year teacher and had heard all the rumors about thrown desks, classroom fights, even police involvement. I'll admit that I was scared to have this 16-year-old freshman in my English 1 class as a repeater, yet this was my roster and this was my time. I was resigned to do my very best and determined to understand this kid and find the best ways to reach and teach him.
>
> Throughout the first few weeks of school, Jameson's attendance was spotty, so I didn't have much of a chance to develop a relationship with him; I knew that was

Step 1 if I was to find out who Jameson really was and what he needed from school in general and my class specifically. And then one day, there he suddenly was. He'd returned after his short hiatus, strolling into class way after the bell and blurting out loud mid-instruction, "What'd I miss? Am I failing?" He most certainly was failing—he hadn't submitted a single assignment or participated in any classroom activities at all. I could feel myself shrinking inside. I knew getting him back on track would be a lot, not only for him but especially for me. I squared myself up, however, and remembered my commitment to understand this kid and to teach him what he needed to learn. That was my job and I was determined to help him.

I quickly finished my instructions to the entire class and quietly asked Jameson to get his electronic tablet out so I could help him create a plan to catch up with all he had missed. He loudly responded, "You gotta charger? Mine's dead. It's been dead since the first day of school." With that disruption finally under control, and because I didn't have a spare charger, I improvised and resorted to an old textbook instead.

It was only then that I stumbled across the problem: Jameson couldn't read.

When I realized that, I wasn't sure how to respond, but I did know that I needed to encourage him if he was going to try at all for me, so I took that quiet moment to launch that goal—praise laced with a huge dose of encouragement. I guided Jameson to a short section of the textbook and he mumbled again, "I can't read. Why you think I don't come to school? It's pointless." I then asked him to show me what he meant. I asked him to read those first few lines of the chapter, and he did with good accuracy, only stumbling over the words "diverse" and "liberated." I say *only* because there were several challenging words in the section that many high school freshmen wouldn't be able to read either, but Jameson didn't confidently second guess those like other students might do. I responded, "Jameson, you just showed me you *can* read, and fairly well. I only helped you with two words. Even as a teacher, I struggle with words sometimes. That's normal." Jameson huffed and grew irritated, saying, "Man, no one believes me. I really can't *read* those words; I just memorize them." Sure enough, when I asked him to tell me what he'd read using his own words, he was pretty clueless.

This conversation went on for a full 30 minutes while my class continued working, and actually days after that one. I was intrigued. Jameson was sullen. I decided to jump in. To test the waters, we looked at random passages with simple and complex words, wrote word meanings on a whiteboard, described the idea of a mental movie camera that created images from words, and so much more. I read to him. He stumble-read to me. I kept praising and encouraging even after he was tired and I was more tired.

All that brought me to a deeper understanding of Jameson's deficiency: he didn't understand the basic phonics of reading, which told me he was really lost when it came to the much more advanced skills of comprehension, summary, sentence construction, and word meanings. He simply memorized words. Really? In high school? I knew I needed to test that out, so I challenged him to talk to me about it openly and honestly. Finally, when I accepted it and asked him if memorizing words was his only reading strategy, he almost smiled saying, "You get it! You actually get it! I've just always memorized words, so I don't get yelled at in school or at home. I really don't know how to read something myself that I've never seen before. Memorizing ain't reading. I wanna be able to really read like everybody else."

So there I was in a room full of proficient students working with this 16-year-old young man who, contrary to public reputation, *wanted* to achieve and really wanted to learn to read, and read well. We revised our plan and started working. The first thing I did was recognize that even though I was an English major and an English teacher, I had no idea how to teach this adolescent to read; I needed help. I reached out to our reading specialist who enthusiastically came on board with a great deal of aid for Jameson and many suggestions for me. Oh, we practiced. We practiced. And we practiced some more. Jameson was starting to *read*, and as a result was developing an academic confidence he'd never really had before. Now there was still, of course, some aggression and some over-the-top energy when he was working. He always wanted to be moving, walking, talking, doing. But we worked on appropriate classroom behavior in addition to his newfound academic skills, and that began to pay off too. His efforts were noticed by his classroom peers, and they began to pull him in as well.

Finally, a few months into the semester, we began a class novel study, and he participated because he was able to comprehend the text to the extent that he could actually relax and enjoy it. In response, I started letting Jameson read wherever he pleased. If it was lying on the floor, he laid on the floor. If it was standing at my spare podium, he stood there to read. If it was doing exercises in the corner, well … let me share how that played out!

One day while I was reading aloud to the class with Jameson attentively following along, I noticed some movement out of my periphery, but I didn't look up from my book because the entire class was pleasantly focused on the novel I was reading to them from. I suddenly realized that I was hearing new voices in our space, however, so I marked my place and glanced up. Oh no! It was my principal and a new leader from the district office, you know, the kind you need to impress. There they were, walking through and observing student learning, and they'd chosen my classroom for their next stop.

At the same moment that I looked up to see them, I also saw clearly the movement I had previously ignored: It was Jameson, arm curling his chair in one hand, following along with his novel in the other. Even though I had stopped reading, he had not stopped chair lifting. He continued reading despite the visitors—I'm not even sure he actually saw them because he was so engrossed in his book. He was *reading* and he was enjoying it.

Because my administrator had spent plenty of time with Jameson during all those past office referrals, she knew how monumental this growth was for him. She gave me a huge smile and whispered to the district leader, "I'll explain outside." I was initially a nervous wreck; I mean, who wouldn't be nervous with a district administrator and your principal in your classroom watching your student doing furniture curls in the corner? It only took a moment for my nerves to surrender to my pride, however. This once disruptive, aggressive student had grown into a focused and pretty enthusiastic learner, in great part because I had taken the time to dig beneath his rough exterior to find the proud young man inside of him. There is power in conversation, in building relationships, in creating caring connections with your students as you ask questions, spending time getting to know them, and showing them you value them as individuals and that you are listening to them, really listening.

At the end of our initial conversation, the one where I discovered Jameson's reading gaps, he told me this: "You know, you're the first teacher in my life to sit down and talk to me, really talk to me and try to figure this out. The first one in my life. Thanks." Those sorts of conversations change lives—for both students and teachers; I know it made me a much wiser person.

In her narrative, Madison describes the connection she created with Jameson, a student who was struggling both academically and personally. His confidence ran low while his frustration with schooling soared. When assessing Jameson's reading, Madison began by asking him to evaluate his own learning gaps, the possible origins of those gaps, and the role of school in his life—what he needed and what he was willing to give in return. She then solicited help for him while providing ongoing, supportive feedback in her classroom; all of this empowered Jameson to improve his reading skills and enabled him to gain confidence in his academic abilities. The most important aspects of Madison's responsiveness, however, may have been her belief in Jameson's capacity to grow and her patience in nurturing that growth, enabling his breakthrough moments.

These dynamics—understanding students, appreciating their cultural context, emphasizing voice and choice, drawing on their interests and talents—illustrate the power of teaching in sync with development. In Madison's narrative, we can see growth in the strength of Jameson's Internal Assets. His achievement motivation increased. He became more engaged in learning. He read for pleasure more often. He reported reading more at home, and, though not overtly stated, she likely strengthened his positive bond with school. Jameson's evolving identity, his enthusiasm, and his growing powers of metacognition brought energy to his learning and increased his engagement with reading and writing. Teachers like Madison conscientiously invest time and effort in learning more about their students, and they encourage their students to learn more about themselves. They clearly understand that students often bring intellectual and emotional uncertainties to a new school year and that creating a safe and supportive classroom climate is essential for their learning.

A Framework for Teaching Well with Adolescent Learners

Madison's report of her efforts to create connections with Jameson illustrates many of the dynamics of successful teaching we have highlighted in this chapter. Teaching well begins with understanding and supporting the developmental changes students are experiencing. This understanding guides teachers in developing positive relationships with students. To integrate support for students with academic content, successful teachers draw from research on good teaching and on the wisdom of practice that stems from thoughtful reflection. Figure 1.3 presents a summary framework that integrates what we know about teaching well with adolescent learners.

In the chapters that follow, we will elaborate on these essential dynamics of teaching in sync with development. To provide real-world examples of ways teachers have responded to developmental issues, we feature additional classroom narratives written by practicing teachers to illustrate the successes and struggles they have experienced. We will share concrete examples of responsive teaching practices that guide understanding of academic concepts. We will show how an essential element of teaching well is assuring the necessary conditions for a *threshold of engagement*, symbolized in Figure 1.3 by a circle that represents classroom communities that nurture trust and collaboration. We emphasize

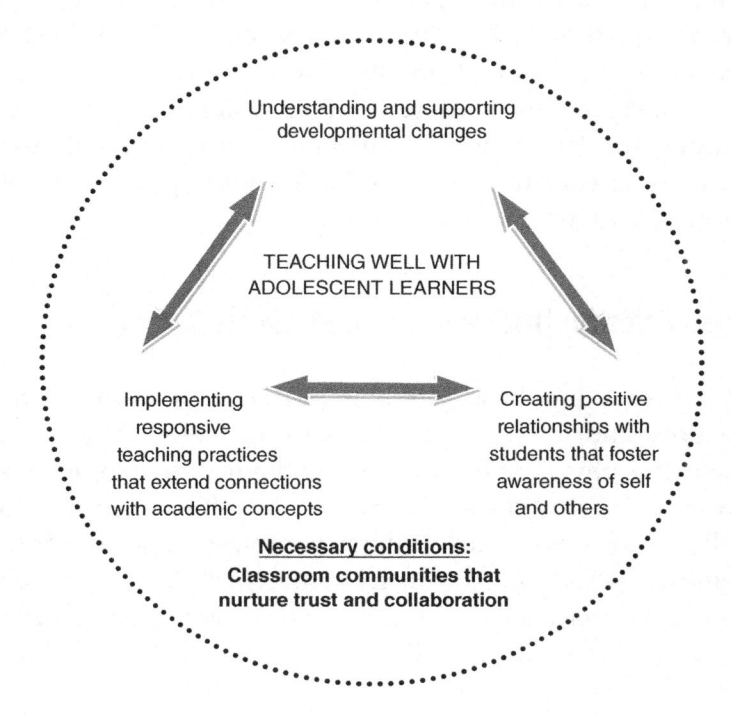

Figure 1.3 A framework for teaching well with adolescent learners

this threshold based on one of the most important insights we have drawn from our case studies with successful teachers.

> Teachers begin by creating classroom communities that invite trusting relationships. They make a conscious effort to learn more about students as individuals and to promote positive relationships among classmates. In doing so, they create climates that promote trust. Trusting teachers and peers creates a "threshold" that invites students to engage more intensively with lesson activities.
> (Kronenberg & Strahan, 2010, p. 80)

This threshold is essential to success. Trusting and valuing students becomes the culture of inviting classrooms. From the beginning, students sense that their teachers value them. With time, they begin to value each other.

The rest of this book will elaborate on and illustrate this framework. Our focus on the positive aspects of development, the strengths students bring to classroom experiences, and the passions shared by successful teachers in their learning do not blind us from the harsh realities some teachers and students face, however. We realize that pressures to maintain safe spaces, improve test scores, and engage weary colleagues create moments of fatigue and frustration. In our final chapter, we will explore these realities and share suggestions for finding energy in collaboration and advocating for support.

Activities for Understanding Students Better

Chapter 1 emphasizes the importance of tapping the energy and talents adolescents bring to the classroom, which begins with understanding them as developing individuals. This closing section of Activities, common to all chapters in this text, offers examples of specific strategies that will assist you in your efforts to learn more about your adolescent students, enabling you to identify and appreciate the gifts they bring.

Intentional Listening

Perhaps the most powerful way to understand students better is to listen intentionally. Careful listening can occur naturally throughout the day or we can make plans to listen proactively. A good example of a systematic, carefully planned approach to listening is the Listening to Our Teens project in Asheville, NC. In the fall of 2008, the Asheville City Schools Foundation and nine partner organizations conducted a Listening Project. Using basic methodology developed in other Listening Projects created by Rural Southern Voices for Peace (RSVP), more than 40 community volunteers were trained to conduct interviews with middle school and high school students and their parents. Sixty-five students participated. Analysis of their responses showed that they felt best about themselves in school when they experienced academic accomplishment, support for learning, positive adult–student relationships, and physical and emotional safety (Strahan et al., 2010). Students perceived benefits of extracurricular activities in general and community service in particular. Although responses related to school were generally positive, students and parents reported several concerns. Students wanted more activities that were engaging; parents wanted better communication.

Results from the Listening Project encouraged community and school leaders to collaborate more intensively to provide support for young adolescents' social well-being and success in school. The *In Real Life after School Program* (IRL) that resulted from this commitment has now been operating continuously since 2010. As described on its website (https://www.acsf.org/irl)

> IRL provides high quality, hands-on, equitable, and accessible after-school programming for all Asheville City Schools middle school students. IRL offers scholarships available to students/families. IRL partners with Asheville City Schools

transportation to provide busing around the city and in the evenings to increase access for students and families. By partnering with 30+ community organizations and professionals, IRL has developed unique youth-informed programs to meet the demands of Asheville City Schools' middle school students.

We encourage you to visit the IRL website for more information: https://www.acsf.org/irl.

This sort of intentional observation can be meaningful on a smaller scale as well. As individuals or teams, teachers can plan to set aside time to interview students, individually or in small groups. Here is a sample of questions from the Listening to Our Teens project:

- When do you feel most successful in school?
- What types of lesson activities do you find most engaging?
- What aspects of school seem to be the most difficult?
- How would you like to change your school?
- What do you usually do after school?
- When do you feel most successful outside of school?
- When do you feel the safest? Least safe?
- Why do you think some students worry about violence and some don't?
- What might make our city (school, neighborhood) a better place for young people to live?
- What do you want to be doing at 20 years old?
- What do you think you will need to know and do to be able to do that?

Using these questions and others, teachers can readily incorporate listening inquiries into the flow of lesson activities. Possibilities might include journal entries, warm-up discussions, current events, team building—almost any Social and Emotional Learning enrichment emphasis.

Surveys of Learning Preferences

Teachers have developed many different surveys and questionnaires to gather information from their students about their perceptions of how they learn best, with many more available on the internet. Here is one we think works well to open conversations with students about ways to learn.

> Learning Preferences Self-assessment Questionnaire Updated from Strahan, D. (1997). Mindful Learning: Teaching Self-Discipline and Academic Achievement. Durham, NC: Carolina Academic Press.

Directions: Pretend that your teacher has assigned your science class a project to research a topic related to adolescent development. She has asked you to let her know how you would prefer to get started and how you want to organize presentations.

Please use the following scale to rate the options:

      1—I would definitely choose this.
      2—I might choose this.
      3—I would not choose this.

Part 1 Gathering Information

Rate each of the following ways you might begin learning more about adolescent development.

    _____1. Searching the internet for articles about adolescent development and making notes.

    _____2. Developing a survey about growing up and using it to get information from students in your school about their experiences.

    _____3. Getting a list of questions from the teacher and looking up answers in the books she provides.

    _____4. Listening to a speaker on the Internet give a talk about today's adolescents (a TED talk or Podcast, for example).

_____5. Interviewing classmates or students in upper grades about their experiences growing up.

Part 2 Sharing Results
After you have gathered information, your teacher asks you to develop a presentation. Rate each of the following ways you might organize and share your information.
_____ 6. Write a report to explain your results.
_____7. Make a poster with drawings that show your results.
_____8. Create a PowerPoint, Prezi, or some other technology-based way to show your results through images and text.
_____9. Write a skit that shows your results.

Part 3 Interpreting Responses
Look back over your responses to questions 1–9 and think about yourself as a learner. When given a choice, how do you like to make sense of information? Select your first preference and put a 1 in front of it, then make your second preference and mark it 2 and so on.
_____reading
_____writing
_____listening
_____analyzing data
_____using visual images (pictures and videos) and objects (manipulatives and other stuff)
_____ talking with people

When you think about the activities you selected—would you rather work by yourself or with others?
_____work by myself
_____work with a partner
_____work with a small group (four or five students)

Please tell us anything else you would like your teachers to know about how you learn best.

Content Area Mini-Lessons That Focus on Learning Preferences

Another way to learn more about students' learning preferences and encourage conversations about ways of learning is to plan short lessons (20–30 minutes) that focus on a concept from the curriculum and feature one primary way of learning. For example, the *Learning Preferences Self-Assessment Questionnaire* is organized around six ways of learning:

- Reading
- Writing
- Listening
- Analyzing data
- Using visual images and objects
- Talking with people

A teacher might extend the discussion of students' self-assessments by planning a lesson that emphasizes vocabulary terms and asks students to draw representations. They could then reflect on what they learned and how well the drawings helped them. Another possibility might be a mini-lesson in science in which a teacher uses representations of the planets and the sun (balls of different sizes) to show distances and relative size. Students could reflect on how well the concrete representations helped them understand the concepts. To organize feedback from mini-lessons systematically, teachers might use a brief questionnaire such as this one:

Student Questionnaire for Mini-lessons
Topic: _____ Type of activity: _____

1. Write two or three sentences that tell what you learned in this lesson.
2. How well did this type of activity help you learn what you learned? (circle one)
   very well   somewhat   not at all

References

Benson, P. L., Leffert, N., Scales, P. C., & Blyth, D. A. (1998). Beyond the "Village" Rhetoric: Creating Healthy Communities for Children and Adolescents. *Applied Developmental Science*, 2, 138–159.

Binkley, R., Keiser, M., & Strahan, D. (2011). Connected Coaching: How Three Middle School Teachers Responded to the Challenge to Integrate Social Studies and Literacy. *The Journal of Social Studies Research*, 35(2), 131–162.

Bishop, P., & Harrison, L. (2021). *The Successful Middle School: This We Believe*. Columbus, OH: The Association for Middle Level Education.

Goddard, R.D., Tschannen-Moran, M., & Hoy, W.K. (2001). A Multilevel Examination of the Distribution and Effects of Teacher Trust in Students and Parents in Urban Elementary Schools. *The Elementary School Journal*, 102(1), 3–17.

Kronenberg, J. & Strahan, D. (2010). Responsive Teaching: A Framework for Inviting Success With Students Who "Fly Below The Radar" in Middle School Classrooms. *Journal of Invitational Theory and Practice*, 16, 77–86.

National Academies of Sciences, Engineering, and Medicine. (2019). *The Promise of Adolescence: Realizing Opportunity for All Youth*. Washington, DC: The National Academies Press. https://doi.org/10.17226/25388

Roehlkepartain, E.C. (2015). *25 Years of Developmental Assets: Personal Reflections (and a Little Data)*. Minneapolis, MN: Search Institute.

Roehlkepartain, E., Pekel, K., Syvertsen, A., Sethi, J., Sullivan, T., & Scales, P. (2017). *Relationships First: Creating Connections That Help Young People Thrive*. Minneapolis, MN: Search Institute. Retrieved from http://page.search-institute.org/relationships-first5

Scales, P.C., Benson, P.L., Leffert, N., & Blyth, D.A. (2000). Contribution of Developmental Assets to the Prediction of Thriving Among Adolescents. *Applied Developmental Science*, 4, 27–46.

Schon, D.A. (1983). *The Reflective Practitioner: How Professionals Think in Action*. New York, NY: Basic Books.

Search Institute. (2003). Boosting Student Achievement: New Research on the Power of Developmental Assets. *Search Institute Insights & Evidence*, 1, 1.

Search Institute. (2018a). *Data Sheet: Developmental Assets among U.S. Youth: 2018 Update*. https://www.search-institute.org/wp-content/uploads/2018/01/DataSheet-Assets-x-Gender-2018-update.pdf

Search Institute. (2018b). *Data Sheet: Developmental Assets among U.S. Youth: 2018 Update*. https://www.search-institute.org/wp-content/uploads/2018/01/DataSheet-Assets-x-Race-Ethnicity-2018-update.pdf

Search Institute. (2018c). *Data Sheet: Developmental Assets among U.S. Youth: 2018 Update*. https://www.search-institute.org/wp-content/uploads/2018/01/DataSheet-Assets-x-LGBT-2018-update.pdf

Smith, T. W., & Strahan, D. (2004). Toward a Prototype of Expertise in Teaching: A Descriptive Case Study. *Journal of Teacher Education*, 55(4), 357–371.

Strahan, D., Smith, T., McElrath, M., & Toole, C. (2001). Connecting Caring and Action: Teachers Who Create Learning Communities in their Classrooms. In T. Dickinson (Ed.), *Reinventing the Middle School* (96–116). New York, NY: Routledge Press.

Strahan, D., & Layell, K. (2006). Connecting Caring and Action Through Responsive Teaching: How One Team Accomplished Success in a Struggling Middle School. *The Clearing House*, 9(3), 147–154.

Strahan, D., Faircloth, C. V., Cope, M., & Hundley, S. (2007). Exploring the Dynamics of Academic Reconnections: A Case Study of Middle School Teachers' Efforts and Students' Responses. *Middle Grades Research Journal*, 2(2), 19–41.

Strahan, D., Buckley, J., Callaghan, P., Pett, K., Woody, H., & Worley, S. (2010). We Can Hear You Now: Results From a Community Listening Project with Middle School Students and Parents. Paper presented at the American Educational Research Association, Denver, CO, May 2010.

Strahan, D. (2013). Understanding Learners: From Confusion About Learners to Clear Understanding of Learner Characteristics. In K. Roney and R. Lipka (Eds.). *Middle Grades Curriculum: Voices and Visions of the Self-Enhancing School*. Greenwich, CT: Information Age Publishing Inc., 213–226.

For Additional Information

Bieg, S.R., Rickelman, R.J., Jones, J.P., & Mittag, W. (2013). The Role of Teachers' Care and Self Determined Motivation in Working with Students in Germany and the United States. New York, NY: International Journal of Educational Research.

Howell, P., Faulkner, S., Jones, J.P., & Carpenter, J., Ed. (2018). *Preparing Middle Level Educators for 21st Century Schools: Enduring Beliefs,*

Changing Times, Evolving Practices. AERA Research Handbook Series, Middle Level SIG. Charlotte, NC: Information Age Press.

Howell, P., Carpenter, J., & Jones, J.P. (March 2013). School Partnerships and Clinica Preparation at the Middle Level. Columbus, OH: *Middle School Journal*.

Jones, J.P., & Hancock, D.R. (2005). *Opening doors Through Enhanced Decision-Making Skills: Preparing Young Adolescents For Healthy Futures*. In D.R. Hancock, L. Lafortune, and P.A. Doudin (Eds.). *Emotions in Learning*. F. Pons, Aalborg Universitetsforlag.

Matthews, C., Strahan, D.B., Cooper, J.E., Merritt, S., & Ponder, G. (2004). Heralded High Schools in North Carolina. *Snapshots: The Specialist Schools Trust Journal of Innovation in Education*, 2(2), 19–22.

Nichols, D., Jones, J.P., & Hancock, D. (2003). Teachers' Influence on Goal Orientation: Exploring the Relationship Between Eighth Graders' Goal Orientation, Emotional Development, Perceptions of Learning, and Teachers' Instructional Strategies. *Reading Psychology*, 1(4).

Ponder, G., & Strahan, D., (2005). Editors. *Deep Change: Reforming Schools for Significance AND Test Success*. Greenwich, CT: Information Age Publishing Inc., Research on Curriculum and Instruction Series, O.L. Davis, Jr., Series Editor.

Salas, S., Jones, J., Fitchett, P., Kissau, S., & Perez, T. (September 2013). Habla con ellos/Talk to Them: Latina/os, Achievement, and the Middle Grades. *Middle School Journal*, 45(1), 18–23.

Strahan, D. (2003). General Patterns and Particular Pictures: Lessons Learned From Reports From "Beating The Odds" Schools. *Journal of Curriculum and Supervision*, 18(4), 296–305.

Strahan, D., & Hedt, M. (2009). Teaching and Teaming More Responsively: Case Studies in Professional Growth at the Middle Level. *RMLE Online—Research in Middle Level Education*, 32(8).

Strahan, D., Geitner, M., and Lodico, M. (2010). Collaborative Professional Development Toward Literacy Learning in a High School Through Connected Coaching. *Teacher Development*, 14(4), 519–532.

Strahan, D., Kronenberg, J., Burgner, R., Doherty, J., & Hedt, M. (2012). Differentiation in Action: Developing a Logic Model For Responsive Teaching In An Urban Middle School. *Research in Middle Level Education Online*, 35(8).

Strahan, D., Hansen, K., Meyer, A., Buchanan, R., & Doherty, J. (2017). Integrating Mindset Interventions With Language Arts Instruction: An Exploratory Study With Seventh Grade Students. *RMLE Online*, 40(7), 1–15, DOI: 10.1080/19404476.2017.1349986

Wood, K., Jones, J., Stover, K., & Polly, D. (September 2011). STEM Literacies; Integrating Reading, Writing, and Technology in Science and Mathematics. *Middle School Journal*, 43(1), 55–62.

2

Growing and Changing
Patterns of Physical and Sexual Development

As we emphasized in the first chapter, teaching well begins with understanding and supporting the developmental changes students are experiencing. Our framework connects this understanding with responsive teaching practices, positive relationships with students, and classroom communities that nurture trust and collaboration. Perhaps the most visible changes to consider are those obvious ones that we notice as students physically grow from children into young adults. Let us consider a few typical scenarios to illustrate this point:

> As the sun begins to set over the freshly lined football field at the local high school, the stands and grassy gathering areas steadily fill with students of all ages. Most are dressed head to toe in school spirit gear, eager to see their friends for the first time since school let out in May. Some haven't changed a bit over the summer, and others look as if they're completely different people.
>
> Take Michael and Ben, for example. When Michael left sixth grade in May, he stood a pretty typical 5 feet 1 inches tall. His neighbor and childhood friend, Ben, an eighth grader at the time, was about the same size at 5 feet 3 inches. Though he was just barely taller than Michael was, Ben had always taken

secret pride in those couple of inches because he felt sure they visually proved his seniority in their friendship, age difference aside. And now here they were, together at the game for their first meet-up since summer vacation began. Michael had spent those intervening months in Nevada with his older cousins, while Ben stayed around the neighborhood, spending time at the community pool with his family, not really recognizing how little his height had changed since the boys parted ways.

Ben realizes his lack of growth pretty quickly, though, when he sees his younger seventh-grade friend grinning and towering over him at the game. Ben suddenly finds himself feeling embarrassed at his shorter height, noticing that not only is he now shorter than his middle school friend is, but he also is shorter than some of the girls in his ninth-grade class.

Claire and Jasmine are also in the crowd, standing together near the bleachers and scanning around for friends to join. Claire, new to eighth grade, and Jasmine, a ninth grader, are cousins and spend a fair amount of family time together, but they don't really consider each other a friend. There has always been a hidden sense of competition between the two. While they spent lots of time together at family events this summer, it isn't until the football game tonight that Claire's envy and insecurities surface.

Though Claire is an athletic cheerleader at her middle school, she's held onto her baby fat longer than most of her friends. She's always been body conscious, but it's not until she sees Jasmine getting attention from the boys tonight, including senior boys, that Claire really starts to despise her own body. She had noticed Jasmine's physical development this summer on their annual family beach vacation; while Claire wanted to wear a swim shirt over her bathing suit, Jasmine appeared to be flaunting her "new additions" in her string bikinis. Claire wasn't really phased much by the glances from strangers that Jasmine got on the beach this summer, but when her lifelong crush from church, Daniel, a tenth grader—tall, muscular, bearded—seems to fall all over Jasmine at the game, Claire is devastated, a little angry, and pretty heartbroken all at the same time. Why can't she look like Jasmine? It just isn't fair.

Not far from Michael, Ben, Claire and Jasmine, Robbie and Jaime are walking slowly around the back of the stadium, doing their best not to be seen by anyone they know. Robbie is explaining that football games were once kind of fun but now are just a hassle with "everybody wanting to see and be seen." Jaime agrees that sports, cheerleaders, and large crowds are definitely something to avoid in the present tense. "I can't wait until I can drive, so I don't have to hang out with my family at stuff like this. I'd much rather be somewhere with good Wi-Fi."

Just a few sections over in the stands, we find two adults, Mr. Cooper, who has been teaching seventh grade for the past eight years, and Ms. Gilbert, a new tenth-grade teacher who just joined the faculty here at her old high school.

"Wow, those kids seem awfully old to be acting so immature ...," whispers Ms. Gilbert.

"They're actually rising seventh graders. I'll probably have them this year in language arts," clarifies Mr. Cooper. "This is pretty normal behavior and especially at the first football game. I try to come to at least two or three high school games a year, and I always aim for the first one. I really enjoy seeing past students play, cheer, and show out with the band. It's always a lot of fun, and it helps me keep some strong connections with the kids on the sidelines, too—you know. I miss some of them a lot. They teach me so much about life every year while I try to cram a little common sense and content into their heads."

He hesitates, thinking back, and then says, "Truth told, I can remember how shocked I was at the varying degrees of growth and development in my students when I first started teaching. My good bet is that you're going to feel the same way, so keep your head open to meeting the students where they are and not assuming that they're older or less mature or socially confident just because of things like size, makeup, and outward appearance. Those things can be a big mask for some of the issues kids hide on the inside. And don't forget that old adage, 'If you can't reach them, you can't teach them,' so build in some meaningful strategies for forming appropriate connections with them over the first month of school. That immediate sense of trust and classroom belonging are critical for their success ... and yours." With that, he makes a mental note to check in with her, maybe even offer to be an unofficial mentor for the social interpretations that typically come up in free-range places like ballgames. It's the least he can do for a new friend and colleague as he vividly remembers some of the chaos from his beginning year as a teacher.

"Just to circle back to that point: don't assume students' maturity levels based on their appearance. I quickly had to learn that all students develop at such different rates, and it can cause some awkwardness and even body shaming among students. The best thing to do? Embrace the awkward, squelch the teasing when you hear and see it, and remind students of their worth. The kids we teach are going through so many changes, the one thing they need to be reminded of is that the changes are normal, and they are normal, even if they look, act, and feel different from their same-aged peers," he continues. *Ms. Gilbert felt the need to pull out her cell phone and take notes—that was such good advice, very different from some of the college lectures she remembered about lesson planning, mandated testing, and state standards. This is the stuff she craves and needs.*

After realizing she hasn't verbally responded, she quickly comments, "Wow, you really understand these kids. Thanks so much for that advice. I'd love more, if you have any."

"Totally, we should grab coffee or something, maybe even lunch this week on a workday, just a way to break up the day and the planning meetings—maybe bring a sandwich to my team room. It's always good to see where your kids have come from school-wise, and I want you to meet Sally and Shamika, two colleagues who gave me a lot of practical advice when I first started out on their team years ago. They're old hands at teaching adolescents, so I know they'll have some good tips to add to this. What do you say?"

"That sounds awesome. Just text me and we can put something in the calendar."

"TOUCHDOWN RAIDERS!" *screams the sports announcer, and the crowd goes wild.*

This vignette features lots of moving parts and developing stories. There are insecure students, a few confidently developed students, and teachers with different experiences, all aware of changes in adolescent physical and sexual development. Those of us who spend time with young people are familiar with these changes. We remember some of our own discomfort with transitions from childhood, the jolts we experienced when we realized that our bodies were growing rapidly in ways we found baffling at times.

Parents and family members notice that adolescents often feel awkward about these changes. Children who used to love posing in the front of family photos now try to hide in the back. Instead of waking early with hugs, they now want to sleep all morning and are grumpy when they finally get up. When parents offer to help at school, their teenagers urge them to stay away rather than asking them to stay for lunch. Teachers and families alike hear their students use words and tones in conversations that we had hoped never to hear from our children, and we cannot help but wonder how long they would stay glued to their devices and earbuds if we didn't deliberately interrupt them.

These situations make their way into middle and high school classrooms in dramatic fashion. For example, just as we get to the critical part of an engaging lesson, we see developmental over-ride kick in. A boy gets up to sharpen a pencil and needs to shoot a paper ball at the trashcan. A girl turns to see herself in the window's reflection and then needs to adjust her hair. Trips to the bathroom become gossip emergencies. Discussions that begin academically escalate into heated exchanges about fairness and especially the lack thereof.

Learning more about these changes can help us respond to them appropriately and even more supportively. As we witnessed in those opening scenarios, and from the individual adolescent's perspective, these physical changes may bring dismay and anxiety, and often with good reason. Their body parts and facial components grow disproportionately. Feet and hands can grow faster than arms and legs. What were once normal movements now suddenly feel clumsy. Pimples and acne erupt at bad times for some, while other adolescents always seem to have perfect skin. Some need braces. Some have perfect smiles. Perspiration and body odor become noticeable, though never, it seems, to the person sporting it. No matter the time of day or where they are, students need to check themselves in every reflective surface.

Ceilings in hallways become reference points for testing the ability to jump and comparing even that to others. With all this going on, it is easy to imagine that some students are thinking, "Everybody is noticing me, and I can't wait to get off this stage."

In this chapter, we will highlight some of the key developmental patterns that accompany puberty, realities of the unfortunate misunderstanding of these patterns, and suggestions that can help us better understand this driving force of early adolescent development, ages 11 to 16 or so. Understanding and supporting developmental changes is foundational to our conceptualization of teaching well, and the onset of puberty is foundational to all of the developmental changes that occur.

Understanding the Changes That Occur during Puberty

As adults who have matured through all these stages of adolescence, we observe the behaviors of this age group with some perspective. Characteristic behaviors that can result in negative stereotypes about teens are often on display for all to see: the distraction, bizarre eating habits, mirror obsessions, constant desire to move, mood swings, and ever-present hormones. These and other visible behaviors and indicators are all part of the physical and sexual developmental stages we experience as humans. Even so, it is sometimes easy to forget that we probably acted in ways similar to the very adolescents we are observing.

How can we combat the negative stereotyping of this unique phase of life? An immediate response is by remembering some of our own changes and by reviewing the current research on puberty. As we reflect, observe, read, study, and reflect again, we will become more aware of changes, their causes, and the resulting actions we might embrace to support our students and offer our guidance. When we understand changes in the body and mind, we can be more empathetic and provide better educational environments. We can also be certain that students have the information they need to understand these changes and to know with assurance that they are not alone—this is normal.

Figure 2.1 Youthful perspectives

So, what is there to be aware of and understand? In this chapter, we will provide a summary of the most important patterns of development:

- ♦ Changes that occur during puberty
- ♦ Hormonal and physical changes
- ♦ Pubertal maturation
- ♦ Adultification of students of color
- ♦ Fluctuations in energy levels and appetite
- ♦ Changes in relationship to physical surroundings

We will present many of the technical details available to us as those who work with young adolescents. In doing so, we will offer suggestions for strengthening relationships and implementing responsive practices that are effective with middle and high school students and the families who support them.

Hormonal Changes

What really ignites the changes we associate with puberty? The National Academies of Sciences, Engineering, and Medicine (2019) describe the initial stages of puberty beginning with "the maturation of the hypothalamic-pituitary-adrenal (HPA) axis, during which the levels of adrenal androgens (e.g., dehydroepiandrosterone and its sulfate) begin to increase" (p. 27). As this maturation occurs, the increase of adrenal androgens causes the growth of pubic and axillary (armpit) hair. This change to the HPA axis typically occurs between the ages of 6 and 9 years old. The next phase of puberty, called gonadarche, typically begins in early adolescence, at approximately ages 9 to 11, and involves the reactivation of the hypothalamic-pituitary-gonadal (HPG) axis. The increase in these gonadal steroid hormones is "primarily responsible for breast and genital development in girls" (National Academies of Sciences, Engineering, & Medicine, 2019, p. 28).

Even without the technical terminology and labels to attach, we clearly notice the physical changes in our students and recognize how dramatic that growth is. With the changes at the neuroendocrine level of development, physical growth is apparent. Like the students in our opening football game vignette, some take pride in these changes. Some find the changes (or lack thereof) embarrassing. This is why, yet again, we emphasize the importance of making adolescents aware of the changes their bodies will go through and how there is no perfect timing; in this case, one size really does not fit all.

Physical Changes

The National Academies of Sciences, Engineering, and Medicine (2019), in their work entitled *The Promise of Adolescence: Realizing Opportunity for All Youth*, further explain how the aftermath of these changes in hormones produce visible, "signature changes" in body parts:

> These include a growth spurt, changes in skin (e.g., acne) and in body odor, the accumulation of body fat (in girls), the appearance of breast budding (in girls) and enlargement of testes and increased penis size (in boys), the growth of pubic and axillary hair, the growth of facial hair (in boys), and the arrival of the first period (i.e., menarche, in girls).
>
> (p. 28)

It is important to note that, typically, girls begin puberty approximately one to two years before boys. Remember Ben from our opening snapshot? He was self-conscious about the fact that he was not only shorter than some of the boys in his class but also was shorter than some of the girls his same age. While girls, on average, may not grow as tall as their male peers, they do experience this and many other changes months or even years before boys.

While some of these physical changes are private, many of them are readily noticeable, such as hair growth, weight gain, and body odor. Just as mentioned before, some students strengthen their confidence from personal patterns of pubertal development while some feel embarrassed and still others seem oblivious to the changes. Each unique behavior deserves a unique response. Our goal is to ensure that all students are provided with support, guidance, and appropriate knowledge of their body's changes. Bear this in mind as we meet Kayla, a seventh grader whose story unfolds in the section that soon follows.

Pubertal Maturation

As we have emphasized, adolescents move through these developmental stages at different paces, determined in part by the multitude of factors that ignite and set the pace of puberty, including, among others, environment, biological makeup, nutrition, and stress levels. *The Promise of Adolescence* (National Academy of Sciences, Engineering, and Medicine, 2019) specifically highlights the stress that accompanies these developmental changes by explaining, "Puberty-related hormones influence the way adolescents adjust to their environment, for example, by experiencing symptoms of depression and anxiety" (p. 33). Due to the vast and often unexplained changes that characterize puberty, it is critical that students understand and expect this personal pace and the individualized results of pubertal maturation.

The National Academy of Sciences, Engineering, and Medicine (2019) categorizes pubertal maturation in three interconnected ways to better distinguish where adolescents are in their process of maturation: *pubertal status, pubertal timing,* and *pubertal tempo*:

- ◆ Pubertal status: how far along an adolescent is in the stages/process of development during puberty at any given time

- Pubertal timing: how mature an adolescent is in comparison to their same-sex, same-aged peers
- Pubertal tempo: how quickly a person moves through the stages and changes accompanied by puberty

Because no two adolescents are alike, these terms can be helpful when discussing student behavior, noticeable changes, and even the methodologies we utilize to better teach them well. In fact, students can move through all these developmental stages within a single semester, an important notation to highlight when we think back to the vignette found at the beginning of this chapter. In that instance, Ben may soon begin to catch up with his peers; in fact, it would not be unusual for him to grow two or more inches taller, gain a solid 15 pounds, and even begin to show traces of whiskers, all within a few months of that first football game.

These changes can be sources of distraction and anxiety for adolescents, however, if they are caught unawares. In addition to the often-perplexing changes puberty brings, it also causes the beginnings of a clear ripple effect that can have a vast social impact, especially for the students who develop outside of the expected windows of time as both early and late pubertal developers. Students must not only be aware of the normalcy of the changes they experience but also must be supported and encouraged to love themselves during the time of change. They must fully realize that their body is unique and may not develop like others around them, those they idolize on social media, or those they follow in movies and on television. Above all, they must know that this is all okay, very okay.

To highlight the necessity of understanding the patterns of physical and sexual development, we present a narrative written by Jaleisha Hargett, a teacher who is sharing one student's experiences in her classroom. The narrative shows how important it is to understand developmental changes and then make purposeful decisions about those changes. When this happens, aware teachers make a positive difference in their classrooms and in the lives of their students.

Classroom Narrative: Kayla's Story

By Jaleisha Hargett, Forest Hills Middle School, Wilson County Schools, NC

Oh, the joys of puberty ... This can be an uncomfortable topic when it comes to middle school students, especially with the light that I am choosing to shed on it. This narrative will discuss the developmental issues associated with the changes that occur in puberty, specifically surrounding African American girls. As an African American woman myself, I know that our culture is overly sexualized. This becomes a big problem for our girls when they hit puberty. It opens up a world of thrills, curiosity, and a sense of being a woman to girls who were just yesterday worried about playing with dolls and having tea parties. With all the reality shows, social media influencers, music, videos, and such that we crave nowadays, it's easy for these girls to go down the wrong path. In their minds, everything is acceptable because that is all they see. That is all that is thrown in their faces.

Meet Kayla. Kayla resided with her mother, sister, and future stepfather. When I met Kayla, she was new to our middle school. She was well advanced in her physical development. Kayla had wide hips and full breasts, which caught the attention of others around her. Being that puberty catalyzes a cascade of important changes in early adolescence—including the development of brain areas sensitive to social information (especially from peers), this skyrocketed Kayla's popularity around the school. Most of the other girls in her class, or entire grade level for that matter, were not as physically endowed. This led to two things happening: either they wanted to become friends with her because they felt inferior to her and wanted to gain popularity, or they disliked her because they felt inferior to her and wanted to gain popularity. As for the boys, well, they couldn't get enough of her.

From day one, I had issues with her attitude. She was defiant, rebellious, and she always had to have the last word. She was constantly the center of attention for her peers. They were hyping her up based on her looks. After not making a connection with her, I decided to read through the disciplinary file that had been transferred with her from her former middle school. I was shocked at some of the actions reported there in her history. She had been suspended multiple times for performing sexual acts at school, along with multiple referrals for fighting and disrespecting faculty and staff. She continued her fighting, drama, and disrespect at our school as well.

Kayla thought she was grown because others perceived her to be. She was also participating in adult activities. Black youth are particularly vulnerable to being perceived as older than they are, and such "adultification" of children can have life-threatening consequences. There was one incident where her Chromebook was flagged in the system for inappropriate messaging. Now, being the child that she was, she thought that just because she was using her school Chromebook at home on her own Wi-Fi meant the school didn't have access to her computer remotely. She was wrong. The pinged messages were searched. After the investigation was over, she lost computer privileges and had to be strictly monitored when the use of a computer was absolutely necessary.

How could this happen? I realized that just because a young person goes through puberty early, the other aspects of development—cognitive, emotional, and psychosocial—are usually not moving at the same pace. So let me say this clearly: even if a 12-year-old looks 16, they should still be expected to think and act like a 12-year-old.

After numerous parent conferences, Kayla finally started to come around. As a teacher, my goal is to educate; however, that education is not always based on my content area. Often, I find myself feeling like a social worker or a guidance counselor. I decided to try a different approach with Kayla. I was a lot calmer when I spoke to her or redirected her. I was also firm with my rules and my consequences. After being disciplined multiple times for disrespecting me, she learned to control her tendency to talk back. I learned that she was often compared to her older sister. Kayla felt that she was a failure compared to her sister, so I started letting her do things around the classroom that made her feel special, such as passing out or filing papers. Eventually, I was able to break that wall of communication down. At times, she would stay behind after class for a while and we would talk. I learned that she liked to draw. When I saw her drawing, I complimented her. She started participating in class more, and things were finally starting to get better.

Ultimately, I changed the way that I approached her vocally. I became more aware of my tone. I tried to be more soothing. I was sure to keep my distance and keep my hands steady, as I have a tendency to talk with my hands, which can be intimidating and overwhelming to some students. I cut back on some of the sassiness of my personality too. If she needed to be corrected, I would be sure to add in a positive along with "please" and "thank you." For instance, she always checked on her hair numerous times in class and groomed herself. One day during a lesson, I noticed that she was in her mirror sprucing herself up, so I said, "Kayla, your hair is beautiful, and your lip gloss is popping. Take a break from the mirror and read this next section please." That small compliment went a long way. Her ego was stroked, and I now had a student back on task engaged in the lesson.

I made a point to let her know that we had a few things in common. For example, she was the ringleader of the singing crew of the class. They would always have a singing session at some point in my class. During independent practice, one day the group started singing a popular R&B song. Instead of hushing them, I joined them. They were shocked that I knew the lyrics to the song and could also hold a tune. They were even more shocked that I joined them instead of scolding them. Again, this was another simple way to make a connection with her.

Looking back, I feel like I served her well. As a first-year teacher at the time, she was my biggest challenge. Her mere presence could make or break the calm environment of whatever room she was in. I wish that I had been less combative at times. Initially, her disrespect really got under my skin. Since teaching Kayla, I have noticed that it has become easier for me to deal with my female students.

In this narrative, we see how Jaleisha's awareness of Kayla's development sparked a better understanding of her as a person, which led Jaleisha to modify her approach and build a solid relationship with Kayla. This is a vivid example of ways we gain perspective and improve our teaching when we follow our holistic understanding of a student—as a physically, sexually, mentally, emotionally, and intellectually evolving human being—with purposeful and positive action.

Adultification of Students of Color

"The notion of childhood is a social construct—one that is informed by race, among other factors" (Epstein, Blake, & González, 2017, p. 2). While all adolescents are especially vulnerable during pubertal maturation, studies show that there are enhanced biases and inequities in the treatment and perceptions of Black adolescents, as Jaleisha has illustrated for us. In their article "Girlhood Interrupted: The Erasure of Black Girls' Childhood," Epstein, Blake, and González (2017) examined the concept of adultification and how it affects the lives of Black children like Kayla.

In this snapshot of their findings, we see the ways in which survey participants perceived Black girls as compared to white girls of the same age. Respondents assumed Black girls:

- Need less nurturing
- Need less protection
- Need to be supported less
- Need to be comforted less
- Are more independent
- Know more about adult topics
- Know more about sex

Specifically, data from this study showed that "adults view Black girls as less innocent and more adult-like than their white peers, especially in the age range of 5–14" (p. 2). It is also important to note that while this specific survey focused on girls, the larger study was based on additional previous studies about Black males, showing similar findings in relation to the inequitable treatment of Black boys versus their white peers.

Epstein, Blake, and González (2017) concluded, "Adults appear to place distinct views and expectations on Black girls that characterize them as developmentally older than their white peers, especially in mid-childhood and early adolescence—critical periods for healthy identity development" (p. 8). When we allow these implicit and explicit biases to shape our perceptions, we add to the unreasonable expectations that loom over the lives of already vulnerable students. These expectations, met or not, can disturb these young, developing Black students' self-concepts.

The adultification of Black students also influences their experiences, or lack thereof, at school. For example, since Black girls are susceptible to adultification, they may have fewer leadership and mentorship opportunities. They may also experience more disciplinary referrals, which often result in harsher punishments. "Ultimately, adultification is a form of dehumanization, robbing Black children of the very essence of what makes childhood distinct from all other developmental periods: innocence" (Epstein, Blake, & González, 2017, p. 6).

This powerful study sheds light on a deeper layer of puberty that must be addressed—a layer of associated inequities and risks. As educators, we have a duty to take this knowledge of adultification and become more aware of our own behavior and treatment of our students. We then need to take action to advocate for change in our classrooms, buildings, districts, states, and nation. No child should miss opportunities for leadership, mentorship, or learning because of biases that result in adultification and mistreatment.

Recognizing Fluctuations in Energy Level and Appetite

As students navigate complex issues such as adultification and other concerns accompanying puberty, they also experience new challenges related to basics like appetite and energy levels, which can significantly impact their perceptions. While our culture has long supported the stereotype of adolescents who sleep constantly, eat a lot, or perhaps starve themselves, nutrition and sleep actually become real problems for most students. Additionally, in recent years, popular culture has reinforced not only thin and athletically fit bodies but also now celebrates fuller-figured bodies, given the rise in popularity of particular models and celebrities who have, for example, extreme curves, full lips, and enhanced eyebrows. Oftentimes, the images glorified by popular media are not naturally obtainable for adolescents and can even be harmful. These images can cause them to go to extreme measures to alter their bodies to fit their perceptions of what is most acceptable and attractive.

Changes in Nutrition

Perceptions of acceptability and attractiveness often intersect with concerns about eating habits and extreme changes in weight. In a recent study of the interactions among nutrition, body mass, and health, researchers concluded,

> It is interesting to note that BMI [body mass index] and pubertal development were not predictors of health risk behaviors. These results would suggest that it is the adolescent girls' perceptions of their bodies and their general mood that predicts whether or not they engage in health risk behaviors to change their bodies.
> (McCabe & Ricciardelli, 2006, p. 431)

What this tells us is that perceptions determine behavior, not weight, size, or shape, whether the behaviors are perceived as healthy or not. Perceptions can be influenced by a multitude of factors such as media exposure, cultural beliefs, social experiences, and even different forms of abuse.

Sensitivity to physical and sexual changes can lead adolescents, in turn, to become hypersensitive about their appearance. We see this in the obsession with the "selfie," social media postings, an emphasis on popularity, the craving of TikTok video trending, and so much more. Whether they approve of their physical appearance or want to look different—skinnier, thicker, more buff, less lanky, shorter, taller, for instance—students will sometimes go to great measures to obtain their ideal look. On the other hand, some students feel as if they are too far gone and will never be attractive, so they may fall into an equally frightening danger: obesity. It is, in part, our responsibility to help

Figure 2.2 Shared selfies

them navigate these misunderstandings and find firm ground on which to move forward in their developmental journey.

In elaboration on that point, a study examining socioeconomic factors related to obesity found serious disparities in trends related to wellness (Frederick, Snellman, & Putnam, 2014). At the same time that researchers have documented a general leveling in obesity rates, children who come from lower socioeconomic backgrounds actually have increasing rates of obesity compared to their peers of higher socioeconomic status. Some groups are exercising more, consuming less sugar, and eating more fruits and vegetables. Others experience a vicious cycle of poor nutrition.

> According to a recent estimate by the US Department of Agriculture, 9.7% of the US population, or 29.7 million people, live in low-income areas more than one mile from a supermarket, where the only options for grocery shopping are "convenience" stores, liquor stores, gas stations, or fast food restaurants that sell foods high in fat, sugar, and salt. Low-income families are less likely to own a car, and thus may opt for diets that are shelf-stable. Dry packaged foods have a long shelf life, but they also contain

refined grains, added sugars, and added fats. Neighborhoods influence not only food access but opportunities for physical activity.

(p. 1338)

The authors emphasize the importance of education in addressing this crisis.

> Education is linked to both understanding what healthy diet and healthy lifestyle mean as well as how to implement them. Children of more educated parents are more likely to eat breakfast and consume fewer calories from snacks, and they are less likely to eat foods with high-energy content, such as sweetened beverages.
> (Frederick, Snellman, & Putnam, 2014, p. 1338)

As educators, we need to fully recognize that home life, parental education, access to nutritional foods, and proximity to areas suitable for exercise all impact students' chances of being at risk for poor health, limited education, and a decreased quality of life. While we may not be able to impact life outside the school building, we can do everything possible to provide nutritious food and a sound knowledge about healthy eating.

Cafeteria food and nutritious snacks might be a place to start. To illustrate this, Jeanneine offers this personal example:

> *As an eighth-grade English teacher, I was plagued by the obsession of watching my students' food selections in our cafeteria—and mind you, the offerings weren't the healthiest to begin with. The boys primarily ate pizza and chips—lots of both—and the girls rarely ate anything, claiming the latest weight-loss fads as their rationale. Still others didn't eat because (and they didn't know I knew, of course) they were hoarding their lunch money to spend at the convenience store at the edge of school property, often on cigarettes or beer that they conned older students from the neighboring high school or college to sneak around and buy for them. All told, it was a bad situation but not one that I had much control over.*

It drove me crazy.

Now, as luck would have it, it was about that time that my district hired a new associate superintendent, and I learned that he had written restaurant reviews in a prior stage of life. Enter my answer. Sometimes things just fall into place even after you've given up.

I made an appointment with him and asked him what he thought about the plan I was hatching. He loved it, so I swore him to secrecy and started conspiring. This is what we did:

Without explaining why, I asked my students to keep a food diary for five days, recording everything they ate in the cafeteria and while on school grounds in general; this included breakfast, as the majority of my school was on free and reduced lunch, so many of my kids ate both meals in the cafeteria. Once done, we went back with calorie charts and nutritional information and tallied their choices.

At this point, our restaurant reviewing associate superintendent came to my class and gave them tips for writing food reviews, and we discussed what a nutritious meal should look like in light of their developing bodies. They were on fire with the plan! We returned to the cafeteria as normal the following week, but this time they worked in clandestine teams to log in all the choices available and the meals they saw other students aside from our class selecting. Our next step was to write joint, comprehensive food reviews for the school newspaper, complete with nutritional information and calorie counts.

Needless to say, that got the attention of our principal, who took the information to the cafeteria manager and demanded change on behalf of my eighth graders and the whole student body. Was I popular in the cafeteria after that? Not so much, but we did get a salad bar, days without pizza and french fries on the menu, and more fresh fruit options. And best of all? My students were allowed to bring healthy snacks for a newly mandated 10-minute morning social break. Totally worth it!

In addition to nutritious meals and information, students also need emotional and mental support, in and outside of the classroom, if they are to be empowered as they are in that cafeteria example. Informal relationships with students can promote healthy eating habits, positive self-concept, and strong body image. A supportive adult can be critically important as students are mentally and emotionally working through the changes they are experiencing.

Guidance counselors can also be incredible sources of support for students and teachers. With their training and access to outside resources, counselors are in a better position to work with students and adults when heavier issues or adversities arise. It is paramount that we refer students to guidance counselors when they experience hardship outside the realm of our expertise.

We can also be more proactive and involve counselors in our classrooms. For example, we can invite counselors to be guest speakers in a lesson rather than using a video clip on a topic that targets an area of their expertise. We can ask counselors to be audience members for general classroom presentations or invite them to explain social and emotional issues that arise in the literature we are studying in our classrooms. Such low stakes encounters may encourage students to feel more comfortable reaching out to a school counselor privately when they experience difficult times.

Changes in Sleep Patterns

As teachers, we notice exhausted teens who seem to suffer from a lack of sleep, which often accompanies the poor nutrition just discussed. Images of students falling asleep in class have become part of the culture, often in a stereotypic fashion. These stereotypes sometimes limit our awareness of the serious issues associated with poor sleep, though researchers and medical professionals continue to emphasize emphatically the correlation of good sleep to good health. Sleep is essential to clear thinking, learning new material, and mental efficiency (National Sleep Foundation, 2010). As adolescents experience puberty and growth spurts, they need slightly more sleep than adults need, with approximately nine hours per night optimal for obtaining the full physical, mental, and cognitive benefits (Eaton et al., 2010). Many young people report difficulties with sleep, and these difficulties can contribute to inattention, poor emotional regulation, lower achievement, risky decision-making, depression, and obesity (National Academies of Sciences, Engineering, and Medicine, 2019, p. 62).

Given the importance of productive sleep to good health, it is clear that the specific start and stop times of the school day can be an issue.

> As many teachers and parents are well aware, US high school students don't sleep enough. Although no set of guidelines is considered authoritative, a generally accepted rule of thumb is that adolescents should ideally get nine or more hours of sleep each night. Eight hours is considered borderline, and less than eight, insufficient. By this measure, only about 8 percent of teens report optimal sleep, and the majority—69 percent—report insufficient sleep.
> (Willingham, 2013, p. 36)

Willingham notes that while some teenagers discipline themselves to get an appropriate amount of sleep, many simply cannot control their sleep schedules. Some adolescents find themselves taking care of younger siblings while their parents work. Others find themselves working late-night shifts or early morning jobs to help their families pay bills. Still other teens *are* parents, trying to find a balance between parenthood and adolescence. "Poor sleepers may differ from good sleepers in many ways other than the amount of sleep they get—for example, socioeconomic status (homes of low-income families tend to be noisier and more crowded), diet, level of anxiety in the child, and so on" (Willingham, 2013, p. 36).

Students may live in a noisy home, drink excessive amounts of sugary drinks, or have anxiety that keeps their minds racing at night—regardless, we cannot expect adolescents whose brains are still developing to self-regulate their sleep. While we can, and should, teach students the importance of sleep to their physical, mental, and emotional health, we would be naive to think this is the solution to the in-school sleeping problem.

Although we cannot always influence school start times, we can craft our practice around the knowledge that this lack of sleep is very problematic. From there, we can be more empathetic with our students' life situations, and we can ensure they understand the health consequences, changing their personal sleep patterns whenever possible. We can step away from course content and take time to discuss life skills like time management, general organization, goal setting, and the importance of allocating time for those things that are critical to good health, such as an appropriate blend of work, sleep, exercise, and leisure—in other words, the life balance that all adolescents, and their teachers, need. We could experiment with assigning less homework so students can go to sleep earlier, and we can make certain our larger calendars coordinate with deadlines for major assignments from colleagues with whom we share students. Finally, we can create lessons that are engaging and relevant and that get students physically up and moving to limit the temptation to fall asleep or lose focus during class.

Changes in Relationship to Physical Surroundings

While it is common knowledge that adolescents grow in height during this stage of human development, we may not realize that during adolescence tailbones and kneecaps also finish forming, which underscores the need for classroom movement. Even though we may not remember a time when we did not have either of those body parts, we probably can remember times when we were uncomfortable sitting at rigid school desks. Adolescents acquire approximately 40% of their entire bone mass during a three-to-four-year span (Greer & Krebs, 2006). As frequently mentioned, this chunk of time varies for everyone, but educators, parents, and coaches must be especially aware of this massive bone accumulation to understand better the impact of contact sports and the discomfort with physical surroundings that students often experience.

For example, imagine we are observing two classrooms in a high school hallway where students are enjoying a period of sustained silent reading.

- ♦ In one classroom, a freshmen English course, students are sitting quietly at their desks, which are placed in pods of four to create a table-like, communal feel in the room.

Despite the effort at community building, many students are disengaged with their reading and are fidgeting, whispering, and constantly squirming in their straight-back seats. Some students seem swallowed up by the desk, while others look like Giant Alice from the scene in Walt Disney's *Alice in Wonderland* after she eats the cookie that causes her to literally shatter the windows with her extremities—they seem uncomfortable and out of place. Many students ask to sit on the floor, but the teacher believes in tight structure and order because, in her opinion, students tend to be the least focused during this time; therefore, she requires everyone to remain in an assigned seat.

♦ In the classroom across the hall, a sophomore English course, students are scattered around the room. Some are stretched out on their stomachs on floor rugs. Others are curled up in tight balls on top of beanbag chairs. Still others are lounging on a couch or swiveling in a chair. All of them are reading. All are engaged, totally *engrossed* in their books, quietly enjoying the time to simply read. Each student seems to be completely comfortable, yet completely focused on the task at hand. The teacher even has his feet propped up, reading as well.

What is the difference between these two classrooms? Flexible seating. Joellyn Marie Travis (2017), in her dissertation entitled "Student Choice and Student Engagement," provides data to support the positive connection between student engagement and the freedom to choose their seating, rather than being assigned a traditional workspace. To define flexible seating, Travis (2017) quotes the Albemarle School District definition: "At least three different choices of seating for students—so you might see a stool, a beanbag, or chairs that look more traditional but allow kids to rock without tipping over" (Travis, 2017, p. 21).

The key point in these examples is for us to remember that the physical changes of adolescence often contribute to feelings of discomfort in rigid physical settings. Discomfort creates a distraction. However, we can offset some of that by providing purposeful opportunities for students to feel both physically and emotionally comfortable in their learning space. A good place to start is by adjusting the classroom environment. For example, purchase alternative seating such as beanbags, exercise balls, cushions or mats, stools, and standing desks. If purchasing alternative seating options for the classroom is not financially feasible, consider the following suggestions and brainstorm others with your faculty colleagues and administrators:

- *Create an Amazon Wishlist, write a Donors Choose application, apply for a local grant from a civic or other organization like Walmart, or set up a GoFundMe account (all may require administrator approval).* Many people want to support students and educators, but they cannot always do so by volunteering their time or donating supplies at the beginning of the year. Be sure to explain fully why you need alternate seating when sharing your request. When community members, friends, and family know you are trying to serve your students well, they will often be motivated to help fund projects such as redesigning your classroom seating options.
- *Go thrift shopping.* Check out local thrift and second-hand stores, consignment shops, yard sales, and online marketplaces for different pieces of furniture that can enhance your classroom. Refurbishing old thrift items can quickly become new classroom treasures and even after-school student projects with buy-in benefits.
- *Turn it into a Problem Based Learning project.* Students love a challenge, especially if they gain from the solution. Give students the task of redesigning the classroom to meet their needs. Have them draw out a blueprint, organize a budget, create a wish list, determine their plan for obtaining the new furniture, and then assign them to write emails or letters (and later thank-you notes) to request what they need from local businesses or organizations. This provides a real-world learning experience in which they will fully take ownership. High school students can even include a project such as this on a resume. Companies and institutions often look specifically for evidence of initiative and problem-solving in their applicants.

And finally, the 21st century has dramatically underscored this need for physical flexibility in the classroom by adding a pervasive sedentary lifestyle to our growing list of concerns brought on by virtual learning during a global pandemic. Indeed, it is all too common to find ourselves in front of computer screens, locked into an ongoing task or class for many hours. We understand the impact this can have on our own adult bodies, but we cannot overlook the more devastating effects it has on young adolescent bodies that are so dependent on physical movement, mental breaks, social interactions, and sound nutrition for healthy growth and development.

Madison offers this from her experience:

One of the most significant things I have learned from my beginning years of teaching high school is the importance of movement, whether that be in the four walls of my classroom or the invisible, metaphorical walls of my Zoom room. As technology evolves, as restrictions due to global pandemics are implemented, as students choose to learn from their homes rather than in school buildings, we must be conscious of the amount of time we expect our students to sit still and stare at computer screens. Whether they are 11-year-old boys bursting with energy or 15-year-old girls eager to disappear, no one wants to sit idle and work behind a screen for hours at a time. I always consider this when I plan my lessons. Even when in a virtual setting, I encourage my students to stand up and move around their learning space. I often have them walk outside when feasible to read, write, think, create, and move. The more movement, the more blood flows to their brains. The more their blood flows, the more oxygen it supplies, making their thought processes vivid and productive. While comfort is key to engagement, so is movement.

Creating Classroom Communities That Nurture Trust and Collaboration

Awareness is the first step toward improving our teaching practice, but it cannot be the last. As we become cognizant of the patterns of physical and sexual changes that accompany adolescents, we must take action by showing support, proving our understanding, and providing guidance to students. We can also create environments where they feel encouraged and appreciated for their minds and personalities rather than simply seen through outward appearances and bodily changes. As suggested in Chapter 1, these actions are the central dynamics of teaching well with adolescent learners: offering sincere understanding and support, developing positive relationships, and creating responsive practices that are worthy.

We trust the information in this chapter has provided a better awareness and understanding of the physical and sexual development of adolescents, and we celebrate some of the sameness we share. We all change. We all grow. We all develop. We all experience newness. Let us remember that those things can be intimidating for all of us, and they are especially overwhelming for the young adolescents entrusted to our care. Some students are in situations where they may feel they have to face these changes alone, yet no one should be. In the best situations, teachers become significant adults who accept them, teach them, and guide them toward their happy and healthy adulthoods.

Activities for Understanding Students Better

As with Chapter 1, this closing section of Activities offers examples of specific strategies that will assist you in your efforts to learn more about your adolescent students. The section that follows targets a critical part of relationship building: nurturing trust.

Constant Conversation and Guidance: An Open Dialogue Centered on Trust

Adolescents are going through major changes, but one thing can be consistent in their lives: the care they experience while they are at school. Adults who take time to ask every day how they are feeling, and then react appropriately to their responses, show them that they care. There are many healthy and appropriate ways to provide guidance to students through open dialogue centered on establishing and maintaining trust. Athletic coaches, administrators, guidance counselors, parents, custodians, bus drivers, cafeteria workers, media specialists, librarians, technology facilitators, career coaches, art teachers, music directors, university interns and their supervisors, and other adults who come into the schoolhouse each day—everyone can play a critical role in strengthening relationships and contributing to the healthy and happy development of every adolescent.

One simple practice is asking questions. When someone asks us a question in a caring way, we feel valued and appreciated. Asking students how they feel can be a classroom game changer. Appropriate questions come in various forms, depending on the context. Here are a few examples of ways to use questioning to nurture relationships grounded in trust.

- Daily check-ins: this can be done digitally or on index cards, sticky notes, or even scrap paper and can function as classroom entry or exit tickets. Students can answer one or more questions about their feelings, their day, and their weekend, just them. Some may be reluctant to share; others may be hoping for someone to ask them, feeling desperate for someone to care. In the first two or three minutes of class, or before class starts or at its ending, ask students to complete a quick "temperature check-in" survey using some of the following questions or others of your choosing:
  - How are you feeling today?
  - Is there anything you want me to know?
  - Can I help you in any way?
  - How much energy do you have?

- How rested do you feel?
- How productive do you feel?
- Rate your day so far.
- What is important to you today? (This could be a question thrown in randomly or on a regular basis. It could be personal or content related.)

Some students may find these questions tedious, but most will appreciate being asked about how they feel. If students have devices (phones, iPads, Chromebooks, laptops, for example), they can use sites like Poll Everywhere, Google Forms, or Survey Monkey to share their responses with you.

Consider giving students a space to explain their answers to the questions, but do not require answers. Forced responses are rarely as fruitful as those offered willingly are. If students do not have access to devices, they might use a chart with different emojis and with privately assigned numbers for anonymity to encourage confidentiality, or perhaps another strategy you choose. Once we know our students better, we can consider changing the questions to personalize them. As we know only too well from teaching experience, adolescents become bored easily, and varying the questions can help with this issue.

And finally, two closing suggestions to consider:

- Teacher mailbox: some teachers designate a box or bin that locks to ensure privacy. Students can submit letters, questions, concerns, and information to the teacher mailbox without feeling pressured to share. This gives students a space to confide in someone and know their shared information or questions won't be seen by peers.
- Teachers share about their personal life: while this may sound simple, it can actually become a bridge that nothing else will create, as illustrated

by Jaleisha Hargett singing with her students in her narrative above. If we show students an appropriate glimpse into our personal lives, it not only humanizes us as educators but also fosters the critical relationships we so often discuss. When we spend time together and share personal experiences and life stories, connections are made, emotions are felt, and relationships grow. Students often put educators on a pedestal of sorts, feeling that teachers know everything there is to know about their content, everything there is to know about life. As adults, we know this is not realistic, but some students do not realize that their teachers are people too with emotions and life issues to address. Appropriately sharing our mistakes and celebrations will not only let the students know we are human but also remind them that they are not alone in experiencing mistakes, misunderstandings, adversities, and more. Suitable disclosure can create a powerful and unbreakable bond between teachers and students.

References

Eaton, D.K., McKnight-Eily, L.R., Lowry, R., Perry, G.S., Presley-Cantrell, L., & Croft, J.B. (2010). Prevalence of Insufficient, Borderline, and Optimal Hours of Sleep Among High School Students—United States, 2007. *Journal of Adolescent Health*, 46(4), 399–401.

Epstein, R., Blake, J., & González, T. (2017). *Girlhood Interrupted: The Erasure of Black Girls' Childhood*. Georgetown, VA: Center on Poverty and Inequality. https://genderjusticeandopportunity.georgetown.edu/wp-content/uploads/2020/06/girlhood-interrupted.pdf

Frederick, C.B., Snellman, K., & Putnam, R.D. (2014). Increasing Socioeconomic Disparities in Adolescent Obesity. *Proceedings of the National Academy of Sciences of the United States of America*, 111(4), 1338.

Greer, F.R., & Krebs, N., F. (2006). Optimizing Bone Health and Calcium Intakes of Infants, Children, and Adolescents. *Pediatrics*, 117(2), 578–585.

McCabe, M.P., & Ricciardelli, L.A. (2006). A Prospective Study of Extreme Weight Change Behaviors Among Adolescent Boys and Girls. *Journal of Youth and Adolescence*, 35 (3), 402–411. http://search.ebscohost.com/login.aspx?direct=true&db=eric&AN=EJ748287&authtype=shib&site=ehost-live&scope=site

National Academies of Sciences, Engineering, and Medicine. (2019). *The Promise of Adolescence: Realizing Opportunity for All Youth*. Washington, DC: The National Academies Press. https://doi.org/10.17226/25388

National Sleep Foundation (2010). *Adolescent Sleep Needs and Patterns*. Washington, DC: National Sleep Foundation.

Travis, J.M. (2017). *Student Choice and Student Engagement*. ProQuest LLC. http://search.ebscohost.com/login.aspx?direct=true&db=eric&AN=ED580733&authtype=shib&site=ehost-live&scope=site

Willingham, D.T. (2013). Are Sleepy Students Learning? *American Educator*, 36(4), 35–39.

http://search.ebscohost.com/login.aspx?direct=true&db=eric&AN=EJ995905&authtype= shib&site=ehost-live&scope=site

For Additional Information

Heissel, J.A., & Norris, S. (2018). Rise and Shine: The Effect of School Start Times On Academic Performance From Childhood Through Puberty. *Journal of Human Resources*, 53(4), 957–992. https://www.muse.jhu.edu/article/706373

Rousseau, A., Trekels, J., & Eggermont, S. (2018). Preadolescents' Reliance on and Internalization of Media Appearance Ideals: Triggers and Consequences. *The Journal of Early Adolescence*, 38(8), 1074–1099. doi:10.1177/0272431617714330

Salomon, I., & Brown, C. S. (2019). The Selfie Generation: Examining the Relationship Between Social Media Use and Early Adolescent Body Image. *Journal of Early* Adolescence, 39(4), 539–560. http://search.ebscohost.com/login.aspx?direct=true&db=eric&AN=EJ1209031&authtype=shib&site=ehost-live&scope=site

3

Thinking and Feeling
Patterns of Intellectual and Emotional Development

Most of us have spent enough time with children to notice how their patterns of thinking change as they grow. Dave recalls a time when he and his wife Sandie took their son Andrew to visit a zoo. Andrew was a little more than a year old at the time and learning his first words. One of his early words was the name of the big family dog Daisy, an Old English sheepdog.

> *That day at our local zoo, Sandie and I were wandering along, talking to each other about something, not paying a lot of attention to Andrew in his stroller. As we turned into the big cat zone, Andrew pushed up in his seat and shouted "Daisy! Daisy!" as he pointed to a tiger.*

It is doubtful that Andrew thought that his dog Daisy was strolling along the fence in a cage. It is more likely that the tiger made him think of Daisy, and he yelled out the closest word he knew. We know for sure that he made a connection. As children learn to speak, we observe this process continuously. Early words become markers for new words that follow. "Daisy" becomes "dog," "my dog," "big dog," "sheepdog," and so on. Words represent things, then concepts, then ideas.

These connections are the essence of thoughts—associations between familiar and new experiences, relationships between similar stories, comparisons of one thing to another, similar or different. With experience, children's connections become more sophisticated. Andrew soon learned that tigers were distinctive animals, different from dogs and other big animals. When he visited the Cincinnati Zoo a few years later, he saw white Bengal tigers, and he learned, among other things, that there are different types of tigers.

Andrew's exclamation at the zoo as a toddler illustrates much of what we know about how the mind works. We look and listen, smell and taste, feel with our skin, and interpret what we experience by connecting the new to the known. Emotions shape our attention, which focuses our thoughts. Andrew responded enthusiastically to seeing a tiger. That sight prompted a happy connection. He focused on the tiger instead of the bench or water fountain or people passing by. It is more pleasurable to look at an animal that reminds us of our favorite pet. Connections spark feelings. Feelings focus thoughts.

As children grow, the connecting process is less visible. By the time students reach upper elementary school, we must look and listen carefully to interpret connections. As teachers, the more we know about how our students think and feel, the better we can plan and deliver instruction designed to enhance understanding. This process often begins with analyzing familiar patterns of thinking development. In this chapter, we explore the major changes that occur in young people's minds as they progress toward adulthood. We consider thoughts and feelings as integrated processes, focusing on

- brain growth during adolescence
- new powers of thinking and feeling
- relationships among risk, reward, and creativity
- growing abilities to reason abstractly
- ways teachers can support expanding powers of reasoning in lessons
- suggestions for helping students connect thoughts and feelings

Brain Growth during Adolescence

A rapidly growing body of research is showing us how the development of thought closely aligns with the growth of the brain. Over the past 50 years, new technologies have enabled powerful tools for studying how the brain works and how it develops over time. Neuroscientists are no longer limited to brain surgeries and cadaver studies for data. MRI and fMRI technologies have made it possible to study fluctuations in brain activity in real time. While the most profound changes in brain activity occur from birth to age 3, changes that occur between ages 11 and 15 are also dramatic. Neural pruning occurs at a rapid rate, creating intense "neuroplasticity," the term neuroscientists use to describe changes in neural connections that accompany learning experiences.

Studies using these new technologies have shown how connections among brain cells grow more sophisticated. Repeated pathways are strengthened through the process of myelinization, in which a sheath forms around nerve cell axons that enables nerve impulses to travel faster. At the same time, unused and less productive connections are pruned away. These changes increase connectivity and result in cognitive processes that are more efficient and more powerful. Growing minds can now think and plan more abstractly. While the process of neuroplasticity continues across the life span, the transition from childhood to adulthood is the time of the most dramatic growth. Adolescent brain circuitry is especially experience-dependent, meaning that young people are energized by opportunities to explore new interests and gain new abilities.

As neurological researchers have learned more about the workings of the brain, cognitive scientists have explored ways our minds develop. We have learned more about the importance of developmental changes in an evolutionary context. For example, human intelligence developed in a hunting and foraging context (Pinker, 1997). Our ancestors began to flourish when they organized into small bands that could communicate to solve the challenges of their environment. Reading nature's signs and signals, finding food and shelter, protecting each other from predators—these were the thinking tasks that enabled survival.

Eventually, these cognitive skills led to the modes of reasoning we associate with civilization.

In this foraging context, the transition from childhood to adulthood was shorter, yet the developing brain followed the same trajectory as it does today. Young adolescents became more aware of their surroundings and more willing to take risks. These changes made it possible for them to venture farther from home, explore their environment, become more independent, and establish relationships with non-family members. As puberty began, these changes made it possible to seek a mate and begin to procreate.

Now as then, changes to the cortical regions of the brain come more slowly, so cognitive control and self-regulation develop gradually. Together these functions of the prefrontal cortex enable skills of executive function: selective attention, decision-making, voluntary responsive inhibition, and working memory (Fuhrmann, Knoll, & Blakemore, 2015). Executive functions develop dramatically in adolescence with growing abilities that include problem-solving, retention in working memory, and the power to stop inappropriate behavior in time to avoid negative consequences (Crone, 2017).

As these skills are developing, adolescents may experience unpredictable fluctuations in reasoning processes. Until executive functions mature, planning may be a challenge, especially in different contexts. A seventh grader who can construct a detailed timeline of events during the Roman Empire might grow frustrated trying to keep up with the mess of his room. A tenth grader who can map out the sequential steps of a complex math problem might struggle to organize a social event such as a birthday party for a friend.

The exploratory and risk-taking abilities of early adolescence provide a foundation for the cognitive, social, and emotional skills that characterize the final transition to adulthood. As the authors of *The Promise of Adolescence* (National Academies of Sciences, Engineering, and Medicine, 2019) emphasized, these developmental changes in the brain are unique to the adolescent brain.

> Indeed, the temporal discrepancy in the specialization of and connections between brain regions makes adolescence unique. The developmental changes heighten sensitivity to rewards, willingness to take risks, and the

salience of social status, propensities that are necessary for exploring new environments and building nonfamilial relationships. Adolescents must explore and take risks to build the cognitive, social, and emotional skills necessary for productivity in adulthood.

(p. 2)

All these developments enable the ability to think more metacognitively. Adolescents become increasingly aware of how they think and feel. Metacognition is "the ability to be aware of or control one's thinking and understanding so that one can develop strategies to direct thinking toward appropriate goals" (Nagaoka, Farrington, Ehrlich, & Heath, 2015, p. 29). The results of this metacognitive ability are life-changing as adolescents learn to think and feel in new ways.

Learning to Think and Feel in New Ways

Learning more about brain growth during adolescence has made it possible for innovative studies of relationships among emotions, thoughts, and actions. Immordino-Yang (2016) and her colleagues examined neurological responses to a wide range of academic and social tasks. Their findings highlighted the intricate connections between emotions, attention, and memory.

> Scientific understanding of the influences of emotions on thinking and learning has undergone a major transformation in recent years. In particular, a revolution in neuroscience over the past two decades has overturned early notions that emotions interfere with learning, revealing instead that emotion and cognition are supported by interdependent neural processes. It is literally neurobiologically impossible to build memories, engage complex thoughts or make meaningful decisions without emotion.
> (Immordino-Yang, 2016, p. 10)

She defined emotions as "action programs that have evolved as extensions of survival mechanisms" (p. 18). Basic emotions such as fear and love have enhanced our abilities to avoid danger and create communities. Curiosity and interest have guided our intellectual and social decisions. Significant learning involves connections between academic skills and meaningful personal experiences.

As neuroscientists have described neurological connections more precisely, cognitive psychologists have demonstrated that emotions are essential drivers of higher-level reasoning (Kahneman, 2011). When making judgments, for example, we may consciously apply rules and procedures we have learned for assessing risk and reward. In these slower thoughts, we perceive ourselves engaged in critical thinking. We often fail to realize, however, that these processes have been shaped by our faster perceptions and emotions.

> Ideas that have been evoked trigger many other ideas, in a spreading cascade of activity in your brain. The essential feature of this complex set of mental events is its coherence. Each element is connected, and each supports and strengthens the others. The word evokes memories, which evoke emotions, which in turn evoke facial expressions and other reactions, such as a general tensing up and avoidance tendency … All this happens quickly and all at once, yielding a self-reinforcing pattern of cognitive, emotional and physical responses that is both diverse and integrated—it has been called associatively coherent.
> (p. 51)

These connected thinking processes help us make sense of new experiences. Knowing more about these processes can help teachers better understand how students think and feel as they encounter lesson activities.

Risk, Reward, and Creativity

Teachers have long observed the important changes in thinking that occur around the onset of puberty. In their detailed review of recent research, the authors of *The Promise of Adolescence*

(National Academies of Sciences, Engineering, and Medicine, 2019) identified two fundamental processes that influence adolescent thinking.

- ♦ First, the maturation that occurs in the prefrontal cortex enables dramatic growth in executive functioning, cognitive control and impulse management. These changes produce capabilities for improved planning and decision-making.
- ♦ Second, improved connectivity across regions of the brain results in enhanced capacities for self-regulation.

(p. 38)

Among the changes the authors describe are

- ♦ greater capacity for memory recall and retention
- ♦ more sophisticated goal selection
- ♦ stronger working memory
- ♦ greater capacity for self-regulation of affect and behavior
- ♦ using evidence to draw conclusions

(p. 42)

The development of these new abilities is not linear or sequential. As teachers and parents are well aware, the stop-start processes of thinking create moments of inconsistency, unpredictability, and sometimes-dangerous choices. To understand better the inconsistencies of adolescent thinking, it may be helpful to review the results of brain studies examining responses to potential rewards and risks, remembering that some regions and systems mature faster than others do (Crone, 2017).

> At the start of puberty, this system is thrown off balance. Influenced by increasing hormone levels, the emotional areas of the brain are additionally stimulated and become extra sensitive. However, the regulating frontal cortex is by no means fully mature yet. So, the emotional system is hypersensitive, while the regulation system is not yet capable of keeping this sensitivity under control. Not

until we reach adulthood will we be capable of getting these two systems in tune.

(p. 59)

In the day-to-day flow of events and decisions, this imbalance may lead adolescents to focus more on the potential advantages of risky behavior than on possible negative consequences. When adolescents find themselves in a non-emotionally stimulating environment like a structured classroom discussion, they are perfectly capable of assessing risk and reason about possible outcomes, but those assessments may not always transfer into life after school. Warning systems mature slowly. Context matters.

This developmental mismatch of maturity in the emotional and regulatory systems in the brain plays out daily in adolescent life, and teachers become well aware of it when they observe the types of decisions and situations their students place themselves in. Jeanneine's years of teaching were inundated with these concerns. Let us turn there for an example.

Though the vast majority of my eighth graders were happy and fairly naive about the darker side of life, I was always worried about those few who entered my classroom in the fall having openly considered (often attempted) suicide, been drunk (bragged about it), or who could barely make it through the day without a cigarette or a reefer (sideline complained). You know, when you think about it, just about every major social decision young adults make has the potential to either kill them or dramatically change their futures. Let's name a few: drinking, illegal and prescription drugs, smoking whatever, driving under the influence of any of that, riding with friends who do, hitting the streets, joining a gang, carrying a weapon, unprotected sex, extreme social media challenges—really, the list is pretty endless and definitely scary from this side of the desk. Act now; think later.

I observed that first-hand for many years and could not seem to make any headway with mitigating it among my students, which frustrated me beyond words. Enter graduate school. The eventual result was a dissertation study that focused on decision-making in adolescence, and I learned a lot—a career's worth of information from the research I did and the students who spent a full academic year with me describing their social and emotional worlds in serious detail. I learned that some rare students had given a great deal of thought to decision-making and consequences, but most of my young adolescents just relied on the "figure it out in real time and worry about the fallout later" approach. Well, you can see how that most often plays out from your own experiences, either teaching or being a teenager yourself.

Let me give you one quick example of that. Consider a scenario in which an adolescent must make a really serious decision: whether to ride home from a party with a carful of friends who may have had too much to drink or to call her parents to come to pick her up, risking questions about the party and her choice of friends. This is actually a pretty common situation among high schoolers and, yes, middle school students too when their older siblings, neighbors, or friends are those high schoolers.

In the safety of my English class, when presented with this scenario in a discussion of the novel Izzy, Willy-Nilly (Voight, 1986), one of my students, Misty, wrote a reasoned response explaining, "If I was Izzy, I would have gone out with Marco too. I would have considered all the consequences when it was time to leave. And I would have thought about what my parents would do and say because I know I'm not supposed to get in a car with a driver who is intoxicated. I knew not to do that just out of common sense. So considering all the choices, I would have told Marco we could stay a while longer because I know that my parents wouldn't care under the circumstances. Then after a while I would have slipped out and called a friend to come and get me. I think that would have been a very good choice."

Yes, indeed, Misty—a very good choice. However, late at night when confronted by this scenario in real time, and knowing from observation how much Misty wanted that feeling of popularity, well, I was fairly sure she'd focus on the fun of riding around with friends and being accepted by a car full of high schoolers instead. I wasn't very confident that she would have called someone after curfew to come give her a ride home. How could I anchor that a little stronger in her head?

Enter a deep dive into my curriculum and a focused attempt to drill some structured decision-making skills into my students as a way to open the door to abstract reasoning, with an understanding of consequences as the immediate goal. The eighth and ninth grades are like the no-man's land of effective decision-making. Kids have the playing field on which to practice making those tough decisions, but they don't always have the brainpower to reason out the consequences and make courageous choices based on a sense of personal well-being. They need some prodding, and that's where curriculum meets need.

Those things worried me then and they worry me now. Teachers who share my concern might focus a portion of the day on discussing structured decision-making with their students. It can apply to anything from novels and the decisions those characters make (back to my dissertation study and that transfer from book to life) or social studies and historical decisions, math problems, scientific discoveries, situations in the arts and humanities, athletics, your SEL curriculum, school-based clubs, and especially discussing an individualized behavior plan with a rowdy student. Regardless of content or circumstance, the opportunities for teaching strong decision-making skills seem about as endless as the sketchy situations our students can find themselves in.

Let me share a powerful little template that I still use to this day. I ran across it when I was digging into the research I mentioned earlier; I was desperately seeking a planned response that yielded more self-controlled behaviors than those emotional reactions my kids described. I modified it to fit my discussions of realistic adolescent fiction, which I then had students transfer into their personal circumstances. It is concise, easy to remember, lays over multiple situations, and gets the job done effectively. It really caught on with them—and me. See Table 3.1.

Table 3.1 My Decision-Making Plan

My Decision-Making Plan
(using the acronym DECIDE adapted from Durrant, Frey, & Newbury (1991)).
Step 1: **D**escribe the problem faced by the character.
Step 2: **E**xplore different options that s/he considered or should have (in your opinion).
  A.
  B.
  C.
Step 3: **C**onsider the consequences for each. Connect these to Step 2.
  For A:
  For B:
  For C:
Step 4: **I**dentify the best solution (in your opinion).
Step 5: **D**o it. (What did the character do?)
Step 6: **E**valuate the character's decision. Was this really the best solution to the situation or dilemma? What would you have done differently (or the same)? What lesson from this experience can you apply to your own life?

Let's take one step back to Misty and our adolescent novel about drinking and driving. After writing about the book, I had my students discuss some of the responses that their class colleagues had given, and I was surprised—and rewarded—when they, unsolicited, applied the DECIDE model to Misty's response. They noticed that she incorporated some of the logic of DECIDE without listing the formal steps.

And here's the teaching reward part: This prompted an engaging, free-flowing discussion about when we might have the time to follow the steps systematically and when we might have to think quickly about what matters most. Someone even suggested, "When we don't have time, just be sure to think about all the possible consequences before we make a decision and go with the very best one." That one sentence made the teaching part worth it. If we can just make the recognition of consequences, both good and bad, routine in our adolescents, then we're halfway home.

This insight is one we frequently revisited in my classes with other examples of realistic adolescent fiction that dealt with tough issues. (I often selected those novels based on overheard conversations or reported social situations that mirrored their lives—instant buy-in.) Let me close by saying that I was always heartened when somebody would say something like, "Boy, he didn't think that through." It valued my teaching, and it narrowed the gap just a bit between spontaneous emotional responses and the brain's developing ability to consider, control, and, well ... DECIDE.

There are positives to be celebrated in this developmental mismatch also, and we want to spotlight those as well. Crone (2017) describes how the same changes that can tip toward imbalance and inconsistency also enable high levels of creativity. Thinking grows more flexible, divergent, persistent, and systematic, all essential aspects of creative thinking. "Creativity refers to those cognitive skills that allow us to generate ideas, insights, and solutions that are both original and feasible" (p. 35). Behind the stereotypic notion that adolescent thinking is wild and crazy may lie the reality that adolescents can often think more creatively than adults may. Studies of brain function have shown that key aspects of creativity reach a peak efficiency around age 15 and then taper off in early adulthood.

An implication for teachers might be to provide opportunities for creativity within the curriculum and be alert to the potential of students, even those who may be hiding possibilities behind the veneer of being "too cool for school." For example, this wealth of adolescent creativity can spotlight life skills like our illustration of enhanced decision-making as we use role playing, novel discussions, nonfiction situations, and artistic responses as drivers of creativity, curriculum, and dialogue.

Abstract Reasoning

As we have already alluded to, one of the most important outcomes of these developmental changes is the growing capacity for abstract reasoning, the ability to think beyond information that is immediate and concrete, like our discussion of future consequences as part of decision-making. "Adolescents develop greater capacity for strategic problem-solving, deductive reasoning, and information processing, due in part to their ability to reason about ideas that may be abstract or untrue" (National

Academies of Sciences, Engineering, and Medicine, 2019, p. 42). Among the changes that occur with the development of more abstract reasoning are

- ♦ clearer understanding of past and future events
- ♦ more sophisticated long-term goals
- ♦ using representations to frame relational thinking
- ♦ greater capacity for strategic problem-solving

Powers of abstract reasoning grow stronger as adolescents develop more sophisticated mental representations. As we have suggested throughout this chapter, thinking itself depends on mental representations. From birth, our minds make sense of sensory input. We interpret things we see, hear, smell, touch, and taste. We seek to understand the world by constructing images of things that we do not immediately sense in the moment. These mental symbols, or representations, allow us to remember past experiences and make new connections. For example, at the beginning of this chapter we described Andrew's "aha moment" as a toddler when he recognized a tiger as similar to his dog Daisy. After that visit, he may have remembered things about

Figure 3.1 Modeling to enhance representational thinking

the zoo—the sights of some of the animals, distinctive smells, the taste of the ice cream he had as a treat. In those later moments, he could not really see, smell, or taste those things, but he could reconstruct representations of them in his thoughts.

Increasing abilities of metacognition enable growing powers of representational thought. While the general pattern of development is predictable, there is considerable variation in the ways individual students experience these changes. Teachers of grades six through ten recognize a wide range of responses to thinking tasks. Table 3.2 illustrates that variation. Nine students responded to a verbal problem with different types of thoughts.

Table 3.2 Responses of Sixth Graders to a Reading and Thinking Problem

Problem Situation: At a meeting of the television news staff, the weather reporter was told that her material was too dull. That night she made up for it.

"Good evening. Today's weather, as you have probably noticed, is different from yesterday's. If the weather is the same tomorrow as it was yesterday, the day after tomorrow will have the same weather as the day before yesterday. But if the weather tomorrow is the same as today, the day after tomorrow will have the same weather as yesterday. As you know, it's raining today, and it rained on the day before yesterday."

Question: Was it raining or clear yesterday? (*Thinklab*. Science Research Associates, 1974)

Student Responses:

Tom – It's raining because the story implied it.

David – Clear—it said so in the story.

Evan – Clear—because it was clear every other day.

Wendy – You can't tell because she didn't say what tomorrow will be like.

Shannon – It was raining yesterday because the weather is the same as tomorrow and tomorrow is the same as today and it's raining today.

Rob – It will be clear because she said that today is raining and if she had said that tomorrow would be raining she could have said tomorrow would be the same as yesterday.

Christie-

Day before yesterday	*Yesterday*	*Today*	*Tomorrow*	*Day after tomorrow*
*	?		?	*
Raining		Raining		

So yesterday was clear.

Daryl – Clear yesterday because of rain today.

Marc – If today's weather is different from yesterday's and it is raining today, it was clear yesterday.

In these nine responses, we see a range of thinking. We could interpret Tom's suggestion that "It's raining because the story implied it" as an attempt to mirror something he has heard others say—or a recollection of a comment from the teacher yesterday. Evan suggests it was clear yesterday "because it was clear every other day." Marc comes up with the same answer but expresses it in an "if, then" proposition. Christie draws a systematic diagram.

We can infer some possible emotional connections as well. Some students, Marc and Christie, perhaps, enjoy these types of logic problems. They may have smiled when they learned they would be working on one of them. Others might have grimaced and wanted to shy away.

Expanding Powers of Reasoning in Lessons

As teachers, we recognize that many of the goals we emphasize in our curricula—critical thinking, problem-solving, and self-regulation—require sophisticated thinking. Fortunately, we have developed an array of teaching strategies to help students develop those abilities. From the perspective of curriculum and instruction, the language of "deep learning" and "surface learning" may guide us when planning lessons that teach sophisticated thinking (Hattie, 2009; Hattie & Yates, 2014; Fisher, Frey, & Hattie, 2016).

Deep learning demonstrates the fundamental abilities of metacognition, abstract reasoning, and representational thought. These deeper tasks are often our curricular priorities. As Willingham (2009) observed,

> A student with deep knowledge knows more about the subject and the pieces of knowledge are more richly interconnected. The student understands not just the parts but also the *whole*. This understanding allows the student to apply the knowledge in many different contexts, to talk about it in different ways, to imagine how the system as a whole would change if one part of it changed, and so forth.
> (p. 73)

Metacognition becomes a critical aspect in the development of deep thinking. To illustrate the interplay between immediate thoughts and more conscious thinking, Willingham (2009) uses the example of learning to drive a car. Most of us remember how overwhelmed we felt when first learning to drive. There is so much to know—how far to turn the steering wheel, how hard to push the accelerator, how to use the brakes without screeching to a stop, how to look beside us as well as to the front and back. Then as we gain basic experience, we learn how to drive in the rain, the snow, and heavy traffic. After a while, these decisions become routine. We can drive and think of other things—the music we want to play, what will happen when we meet a friend, what to do over the weekend. We can think of these things when the roads are clear, the traffic is moving, and we do not sense a risk. However, when someone stops suddenly in front of us or we see rows of brake lights ahead or hear a siren, we shift from our automatic mode to a careful, more aware type of driving.

As Bernadowski (2016) suggests, metacognition also enables students to consider their learning strategies consciously. From her perspective as a reading teacher, she describes ways that students gain learning power as they take more ownership of their thoughts. When readers learn to monitor their comprehension, they can set purposes and goals, regulate the flow of reading, activate background knowledge, and make new connections with information. She recommends that teachers ask guiding questions that promote strategic learning, such as

- What do you notice about reading when you understand what you've read?
- What is it that causes you difficulties?
- In what areas of reading and remembering do you feel most at ease?

Metacognition likewise enhances the use of prior knowledge in making connections with new concepts in content area lessons. For example, students who know that the Civil War occurred in the 1860s, that the Confederate states left the Union, and that battles killed thousands of soldiers, can immediately understand why dedicating a cemetery at Gettysburg was a big moment for President Lincoln. Students with prior knowledge can focus on studying the language he used and its impact. They have enough information in long-term memory to concentrate their working memory on the task at hand. Students without that prior knowledge can feel like first-time drivers. There is so much information in their learning environment that they feel overwhelmed. Without guidance, they may grow frustrated, tune out, or seek diversion.

A helpful framework for understanding how students strengthen their powers of reasoning and use them to make sense of academic content is the SOLO taxonomy. Developed by Biggs and Collis (1982), the Structure of Observed Learning Outcomes (SOLO) taxonomy is a tool for identifying the progression toward a deeper understanding of academic tasks. As developed by the authors, the SOLO taxonomy "describes the growth in complexity of performance in many learning tasks, from the earliest engagement in the task to expertise" (Biggs & Collis, 1989, p. 151). The SOLO taxonomy provides a system for analyzing progressions from surface level to deep understanding. The SOLO reflects the familiar perspective that thinking grows from the concrete toward the abstract, as well as the equally familiar construct of higher-level reasoning from Bloom's Taxonomy. Stated in practical terms, ideas develop as students first learn individual concepts, then connect concepts into relationships, and finally generate their own creative applications.

The SOLO taxonomy characterizes this progression on a continuum of five levels. At the lowest level (prestructural), responses demonstrate no real understanding of the concept; that is, ideas are not yet structured. Unistructural responses demonstrate one key aspect of the concept. At the multistructural level, responses demonstrate two or more aspects but without showing relationships among them. At the relational level, several aspects are integrated into a whole. The most sophisticated responses (extended abstract) demonstrate personal generalizations and new connections.

To illustrate ways adolescents make sense of academic concepts, we share a streamlined version of the SOLO taxonomy that we have used with teachers in a variety of settings. As shown in Table 3.3, comprehension of a new concept such as "density" follows a general progression.

Our modified SOLO taxonomy provides a framework for explaining much of what we have learned about patterns of intellectual and emotional development. When young children like Andrew first encounter an unfamiliar animal like a tiger, they make a concrete and singular connection with something familiar, like the family dog. As they experience related examples, they associate these as similar. With additional experiences and more conscious thought, they identify relationships among examples. "All of these big, four-legged animals with stripes that look like cats are tigers." As adolescents, they can organize their understanding into divisions and subdivisions of animal kingdoms. New experiences fuel this process as students grasp additional aspects of information and make deeper connections.

Let us stop here for an example that could easily be found in a high school science classroom.

In a unit on density, the progression from surface toward deep might happen in a natural fashion when a tenth-grade teacher plans learning tasks to build concepts. He could introduce the unit with a puzzling scenario, or phenomenon. Asking

Table 3.3 Levels of Understanding in a Progression from Surface to Deep

Level (with reference to the levels of the SOLO Taxonomy)	Description of student understanding	Examples related to concepts of density
No learning yet (Prestructural level)	Has no prior knowledge	"I'm not sure what the word density means."
First connection (Unistructural level)	Learns one aspect or detail	"Ice is not as dense as water so it floats."
Multiple connections (Multistructural level)	Learns several aspects, does not yet integrate them	"Density has to do with volume and weight."
Relational connections (Relational level)	Integrates and organizes information into concepts	"Density is the ratio of an object's mass to its volume."
Abstract connections (Extended abstract level)	Creates personal generalizations and new connections at higher levels of understanding	"Density explains why a boat made of tinfoil will float. The mass of foil is distributed across a large volume."

students to observe carefully, he may show them an aquarium filled with warm water, drop in a large chunk of ice frozen from water dyed blue, and ask students to describe in their notes what happens next. As the ice melts, dark blue water sinks to the bottom, and then gradually spreads throughout the tank. Students record their observations and generate hypotheses:

- Malik writes, "I think there is something different in the texture of the cold water. When it warms up, it blends."
- Gabrielle sketches the tank and draws arrows to show the flow of the blue coloring. "The ice melted and sank to the bottom. I think the food coloring made it heavier."

After asking students to share observations, the teacher suggests that this experiment has something to do with density and writes that word on the board. He then asks students to begin a new page in their science notebooks and give a definition of density in their own words.

- Malik writes, "Density is how close together things are."
- Gabrielle writes, "Density has to do with how heavy things are compared to other things, like a rubber ball is denser than a ping-pong ball."

Next, students work in teams to complete an experiment. Each team receives a clear quart jar and beakers of four liquids: corn syrup, blue dish soap, water colored red, and canola oil colored green. They slowly pour the corn syrup into the jar to form a yellow layer on the bottom. Next, they pour an equal amount of the blue dish detergent, followed by the red water, then the green canola oil. When they put the lid on the jar, they slowly turn the jar on its side and watch. Then, they turn it upside down. Finally, they stand it right side up.

- In his notes, Malik observes, "Every time we moved the jar, the colors settled in the same order—yellow on the bottom, then blue, then red, then green."
- Gabrielle writes, "The different liquids must have different densities because they stayed separate."

The following day, the teacher might ask students to read a brief article that begins with the story of Archimedes' legendary discovery of water displacement and the fake gold crown, then explains the formula for calculating density, and concludes with a chart listing different substances and their relative densities. Among them are:

Substance	Density (grams per cubic centimeter)
Air	0.0013
Wood (oak)	0.6
Ice	0.92
Water	1.00
Steel	7.80
Silver	10.50
Gold	19.30

As they read, students complete a study guide with four questions:

Question 1: Who was Archimedes and what did he discover about density?

Malik: Archimedes (we'll call him Archie) was a mathematician in ancient Greece who figured out that you could test a crown by seeing how much water it spilled out. He became famous for running naked through the streets.

Gabrielle: Archimedes figured out that a fake crown would have a different density than a real gold crown.

Question 2: Define density in your own words.

Malik: Density has to do with atoms and molecules, how much stuff is in them.

Gabrielle: Density is how closely packed in the particles are.

Question 3: What does the formula "density = mass/volume" mean?

Malik: This shows how you can use a math formula to figure out the density of something.

Gabrielle: This formula means that the density of something is the ratio of how much it weighs to how much space it has.

Question 4: Use the formula to explain what you observed in the experiment with colored liquids.

Malik: The yellow liquid always stayed on the bottom so it must have the highest density. We added the same amount of each one so their densities are different.

Gabrielle: Each time we moved the jar, the liquids settled in the same order. Like the things listed in the chart, it shows that when something has a lower density than something else, it floats on it.

This portion of the unit could conclude with a writing assignment using the prompt:

As you learned in the article we read, the density of water is 1.00 and steel is 7.80. Using what we have learned about density so far, explain 1) how a big ship like the Titanic could float in water even though it was made of steel and 2) how it sank.

Malik: I think the big ship could float because it had air in it, kind of like there is some air in ice so it floats, or if you blow up a floatie toy with air, it will float. I saw in the movie that water started rushing into the ship when it smashed into the iceberg. The water added to the weight of the steel, and it got too heavy to float, probably because the air came out, just like if something pokes a hole in a floatie toy.

Gabrielle: The Titanic could float because it had a lot of air inside it. The steel that made the ship was thin, like in sheets, and they held a lot of air inside. This means that the volume of the ship was mostly air. The article said that air has a density of 0.0013 so, if you think about the formula, the big volume of air would make up for the weight of the steel. When the ship hit the iceberg, the water started coming in, and the air left so the ship sank.

In these examples from a sophomore science lesson, we see glimpses of the ways Malik and Gabrielle are thinking. Their responses suggest that they formed deeper connections as they made sense of their learning experiences. Each of them had a general understanding of the term "density." As they thought about the experiments, they used their new insights to make multiple connections. Reading the article provided an explanation of the relationships between density, volume, and mass. The formula for density gave them a mental representation they could use to explain the complicated phenomenon of steel floating on water—and then sinking.

In this illustration, we also see how instructional experiences are critical factors in the development of deeper understanding. The teacher planned a sequence of activities that would guide students toward higher levels of reasoning. He began with a puzzling situation to heighten interest and emotional connection. The small group experiment with liquids provided both new information and time to share thoughts with classmates. He selected a brief reading passage that explained the scientific concepts they had encountered in the experiments and guided their thinking with questions. Finally, he presented a writing task that would encourage them to put it all together in a way that made sense to them.

Expanding powers of reasoning in lessons requires teachers to understand both the progression of ideas in the content and the nature of the prior knowledge students bring to the unit. As Willingham (2009) reminds us,

> We understand new things in the context of things we already know, and most of what we know is concrete. Thus, it is difficult to comprehend abstract ideas, and difficult to apply them in new situations. The surest way to help students understand an abstraction is to expose them to many different versions of the abstraction—that is to have them solve area calculation problems about tabletop soccer fields, envelopes, doors, and so on.
>
> (p. 67)

Using what they know about how students' thinking develops, teachers understand that the challenge is not just providing concrete examples. It is also about providing concrete examples that are familiar to students and presenting them in a sequence that will make sense to them. As Willingham concludes,

So, understanding new ideas is mostly a matter of getting the right *old* ideas into working memory and then rearranging them—making comparisons we hadn't made before, or thinking about a feature we had previously ignored.

(p. 70)

Using what they know about how students' thinking develops also helps teachers personalize instruction. They can tailor their plans for activities to students' interests and emotions as well as their academic understanding. To illustrate how teachers put their knowledge of students' reasoning development into practice, we share a narrative from a veteran science teacher.

Classroom Narrative: Analysis of a Science Unit

By Amanda Clapp, The Catamount School, Sylva, NC

When I read *Mosquitoes Don't Bite Me* by Pendred Noyce (2017), I decided to develop a unit for my eighth-grade science class that featured this novel. The main character is Nala Simiyu, a seventh grader who learns that her natural resistance to mosquitoes is part of her genetic heredity. Her research into mosquitoes and contact with a drug company lead her to an adventure in Kenya. Themes of racism, health care, and biological ethics make this book a great launch pad for a unit.

I planned a series of mini-lessons that would begin with passages from the novel and feature important topics from our science curriculum:

♦ race as a social construct,
♦ ethics in science,
♦ Black Lives Matter,
♦ African economics, and
♦ drug companies.

From our NC Eighth Grade Science Curriculum, I identified the essential standards we would address and generated a standards-based rubric:

1–2 Developing (Remember/Recall)	3 Proficient (Understand/Apply)	4 Mastery (Analyze/Evaluate)
♦ *Vocabulary* ♦ *Disease recognition* ♦ *Describes vectors OR disease transmission*	**I can describe the connection between mosquitoes and disease.** ♦ Describes mosquitoes as vectors of at least one disease ♦ Describes the connection between mosquito bites and disease transmission	♦ *Identifies different mosquito-borne pathogens* ♦ *Analyzes effects of mosquito prevention* ♦ *Creates solutions to vector-borne illness*

♦ Vocabulary	I can explain the variation in human skin color based on recent adaptations and genetics. ♦ Compares cultural concept of race and biological one ♦ Describes variation of human skin as a reaction to the sun	♦ Discusses implications of social constructs and difference from biology ♦ Predicts future social and biological changes ♦ Evaluates social issues through the lens of biology
♦ Vocabulary ♦ Describes diseases	I can describe the relationship between sickle cell disease and malaria in human history. ♦ Describes the inheritance of sickle cell disease and its symptoms ♦ Describes malaria and its symptoms ♦ Explains how sickle cell protects people from contracting malaria	♦ Analyzes overlap between racial groups, healthcare, and sickle cell disease in modern populations ♦ Evaluates change in sickle cell trait over time across the globe

Based on class protocols, I gave students a copy of the "Proficient" column of this rubric and we discussed our three goals at the beginning, middle, and end of this activity sequence. I added the first and third columns to help me flesh out examples of higher-level thinking and lower-level thinking based on a 1–4 standards-based grading scale. At the beginning, middle, and end of the unit, the students self-assessed and gave examples of their proficiency using the rubric, as well.

As we experienced the unit, I conducted several formative assessments. I developed a probe to address misconceptions about disease transmission. Students showed that they understood the role of vectors in transmitting microbes that cause disease. Since they had the basics of this surface-level understanding, I used the novel to develop deeper understandings of evolution in human history by focusing on skin color across humans and by discovering the co-evolution between the sickle cell trait and malaria. Based on these insights and the interests students expressed, I developed two options for final projects:

Student Product Choices

CHOICE 1
♦ Survey the sources and create an infographic explaining the relationship between the sickle cell trait and malaria.

CHOICE 2
♦ Reflection exercise: Write a brief essay that describes a big idea you developed as we explored this book (1–2 pages).
  ◊ What do you think?
  ◊ What happened in the book?
  ◊ What is the science/ research on the topic?
  ◊ What sources do you have?

During the flow of the unit, I focused most of my attention on engaging students with the activities and encouraging them to connect what they were reading in the novel with the scientific concepts. I was excited to see the students so enthusiastic about the book and the mini-lessons. Students who did not often look forward to reading walked in asking how long they could read before we started activities. Students talked animatedly about the characters in the novel and how they reminded them of their friends. And since we included social justice topics in our lessons, the students wanted to share experiences of oppression and feelings of outrage at how the students in the book treated each other. The students were able to show an understanding of the science of human diversity as they learned and expressed that "there's no reason to treat people differently!"

After we completed the unit, I wanted to get a clearer sense of what students learned about science and think of ways to improve this unit before I taught it again next year. I decided to analyze a sample of final products in reference to the three goals of the unit. This sampling was based on the students who submitted their work digitally. Since the students were given a choice of topics, I knew their products would not reflect mastery of all three goals. My hope was to find a pattern in interests and in learning through this fiction-based approach to science and ethics.

My analysis of 18 final products showed that four students focused on the relationship between mosquitoes and disease, seven focused on the science of skin color and/or the Black Lives Matter movement, and seven focused on the co-evolution of sickle cell disease and malaria in some human populations. In all 18 projects, students demonstrated some new connections related to the concepts emphasized. Twelve showed proficiency based on the rubric we developed. Three students did not submit enough work to show evidence of proficiency (James, John, Mary), and three students addressed issues at a reactionary/superficial level, along the lines of "racism is bad" (Patricia, Robert, Jennifer). The other students in class used outside resources and drew connections between change over time and human history.

Of the projects related to variation in human skin color, only one (Linda) talked about the science of skin color with scientific sources. For example, Linda wrote:

> People that have difference skin color than others are considered out of order and out of place on some situations, but in others it is just another person, and they treat them the same because they don't care.
>
> In the book *Mosquitoes Don't Bite Me*, North Carolina has some people darker than others but not as much as there would be in Africa. In the US if you are in Maine, the chance of you coming across a darker skin person is low. Likewise, northern peoples tend to have lighter skin colors because they don't receive as many of the sun's harmful UV rays. But it you live nearer to the equator you still have much darker skin because the sun is more likely to hit that spot of the earth and your bodies are releasing more melanin as it acts as a natural sunscreen by absorbing these UV rays.

Her one-page summary explained the adaptation to sunlight in human populations by creating more melanin. Linda didn't add opinions or reflections; she just used an expository essay to explain human skin diversity.

Of the projects related to sickle cell disease and malaria, only two (Elizabeth and Barbara/Susan) talked about the relationship between sickle cell and malaria with scientific sources. These students finished reading the book ahead of schedule and dove into the first option for a final project, doing some extra research on how the sickle cell trait can protect a person from malaria, but having sickle cell disease can kill a person. They looked at the nature of genetics, and both groups used PowerPoints to illustrate their learning. Elizabeth's final set of slides included the following:

> How is sickle cell inherited? (transmission)—It's a genetic gene that is inherited in a co-dominance pattern, which means both copies of the genes have mutations. Each parent carries one copy of the gene and often does NOT have symptoms of the condition.
>
> Malaria Transmission—Malaria is transmitted by the bite of an infective (Female) Anopheles mosquito. (The most common way) Rarely, it can occur from the transfusion of blood from infected people through needles and syringes. And even sometimes organ transplants.
>
> What does sickle cell do to you?—Sickle cell anemia is an inherited form of anemia—a condition when there aren't enough healthy red blood cells to carry adequate oxygen throughout the body. These irregular shaped blood cells can get stuck in small blood vessels, which can slow or block blood flow and oxygen to parts of the body.
>
> What does malaria do to you?—When bitten, the plasmodium parasite enters your bloodstream. Then it's carried to the liver where it multiplies. In the liver, it matures. After a couple of days, it then travels to the bloodstream again and infects the red blood cells.

After additional slides describing the symptoms and challenges of the diseases, she concluded with the following slides:

> How does sickle cell prevent malaria?—Individuals who are carriers of sickle cell disease (with one gene and one normal hemoglobin gene, also known as the sickle cell trait) have some protective advantage against malaria. As a result, the frequencies of sickle cell carriers are high in malaria-endemic areas.
>
> Miniature Reflection to *Mosquitoes Don't Bite Me*—I believe a significant concept of the book was to understand the severity of different diseases in more rural areas. I found it intriguing on how they went about the process because I haven't seen the behind the scenes in any detail. I learned more about how poverty affects people in their culture and how they go about things to thrive. (Digging ditches for cars that pass) The comparison between the American people and Kenyans was drastic. It revealed some knowledge lacked by people in more wealthy countries to those who struggle.

Elizabeth's project shows that while she focused on presenting facts, she was able to identify relationships among facts and make personal connections with the information she presented. Using disease research as a mode of learning, she was able to make deep connections between privilege and health across the world, and to learn about science and global issues as an eighth grader.

The general pattern among the projects was that most students demonstrated a surface-level understanding of facts and details, yet did not approach deeper or more personal levels of understanding. Their responses may be the result of a very broad assignment in which I may not have given students specific enough parameters. The expectation that they all tie their analyses to the science may not have been as clear as it could have been, and therefore students did not do it. Assessments that are more specific should be incorporated into the unit to give students a more structured set of expectations. Differences among projects also reflect the amount of time spent on their products, as well as differences in reading abilities. Our more efficient readers had more time to spend on researching and writing.

Based on this analysis, the combination of ethics, personal stories, and scientific facts is extremely engaging to students. Allowing them to pursue their interests along any of those lines is valuable, but individual assessments will be important to disentangle the students' understanding of science, society, and their intersection. The way to determine the relationship between skin color and race as a social construct may be through genetics, discussing the complexities of human genetics instead of the typical middle school Mendelian genetics unit. Then, students will have a scientific basis for diversity in their minds before tackling the novel's social issues in their disease unit. Broadening these concepts across units will allow students more time to consider them, more purposeful instruction, and more opportunities for assessment along the way.

When I revise my plans for next year, I intend to keep the hook of social, biological, and personal lenses in this unit. I will use the novel again, but I plan to incorporate more specific human genetics instruction to address the understanding of skin color. The combination of the two sources will provide a stronger base for higher-level thinking in analyzing the inheritance of skin color as well as sickle cell disease, and the evaluation of the social issues associated with those traits. This might also bring in that half of the students who chose skin color and BLM, showcasing their interest and perhaps advocacy of this given our nation's current climate.

Amanda's narrative demonstrates how she thought carefully about her students as she planned a unit and how she analyzed their learning. Like other successful teachers, she focused on engaging and responding to students during lessons. She drew energy from their enthusiasm toward the novel and activities. She collaborated with them to develop project options for demonstrating what they learned. The essays and electronic slide presentations they created provided evidence of their thinking, which she used to learn more about their levels of reasoning. She integrated all this information to develop plans for improving the unit the next time she teaches it.

As she planned her unit, Amanda realized that her students did not know as much about the transmission of diseases and genetics as she did. She thought carefully about her curriculum standards and unpacked her understanding of key concepts to relate them to students. This is an essential process in guiding student reasoning. Like Ms. Hutchison in Chapter 1, teachers often understand their content so well that it has become automatic, and they struggle to break it down to levels appropriate for student learning. Like experienced drivers, they can think about concepts on cruise control, so much so that it becomes almost impossible to remember what it was like when they did not understand. Taking time to examine concepts systematically, identify potential sources of misunderstanding, and then decide how to sequence learning experiences becomes essential.

Analyzing ways that students' thinking grows more sophisticated by processing surface-level information and generating deeper connections helps successful teachers plan lessons that scaffold understanding. With these instructional experiences, students' thoughts grow richer and they become more adept at thinking about their thoughts. This growing capacity for metacognition is especially important in making sense of the emotional aspects of thinking. As adolescents, students are better able to recognize impressions, intuitions, and intentions. With teacher guidance, they become more aware of ways they can exert executive control, harnessing new powers to think more deliberately.

Connecting Thoughts and Feelings

Stronger executive control also enhances awareness of feelings. As we have emphasized in this book, emotional development is a complex, negotiated process. Students enter our classrooms with perceptions of themselves as people and as students based on years of experience. Each new encounter with teachers, classmates, or subject matter triggers a set of emotions. Positive experiences affirm positive perceptions or soften negative ones. Negative experiences reinforce doubts and weaken confidence. Together, these interactions shape perceptions of identity, which then influence the next set of interactions. At each moment along the way, feelings and understandings intertwine and become inseparable as they create our thoughts.

While these general patterns of emotional learning are often apparent, researchers have stressed that emotional maturation occurs in an irregular progression. Hormonal changes and social situations often cause an upsurge in sensitivity. Emotional awareness fluctuates accordingly. As with the more cognitive aspects of thinking development, metacognition plays a crucial role in self-awareness. Being able to think better about thoughts and reactions enables adolescents to make better sense of unpredictable situations.

Growing powers of metacognition also make possible greater awareness of personal interests and passions. Students often find activities that engage them intensely, like music, art, sports, video games, and reading. A useful framework for understanding how they integrate thinking and feeling into these activities is Flow Theory.

Csikszentmihalyi (1990) first proposed Flow Theory more than 30 years ago. As a psychologist, he began his research with a focus on happiness: what makes us happy and what happens in our minds when we are happy? In his interviews with successful people who appeared to be happy in their work, he noticed that they found it difficult to talk about happiness as an abstraction. Instead, they talked in detail about the activities that engaged them. Artists were compelled to paint or sculpt. Musicians spent hours practicing, and loved it. Successful athletes, writers, and hobbyists all shared one characteristic: they became so engaged with activities that they lost track of time. Csikszentmihalyi called this state of mind "flow."

> Flow is what people feel when they enjoy what they are doing, when they would not want to do anything else. What makes flow so intrinsically motivating? The evidence suggests a simple answer: in flow, the human organism is functioning at its fullest capacity. When this happens, the experience is its own reward.
> (Csikszentmihalyi & Nakamura, 1989, p. 55)

Figure 3.2 "My soccer goals," digital art by Ellie C.

Csikszentmihalyi and his colleagues found that participants shared stories of being so engaged with the moment at hand that they forgot to take a break to eat, or they even failed to remember something important they were supposed to do. These moments of immersion characterize flow as one of the most powerful states of mind, one in which thoughts and feelings merge seamlessly.

One of their most intensive studies examined the daily life of adolescents over a 12-year period. The resulting analysis identified more than 100 different activities that adolescents viewed as enjoyable. Csikszentmihalyi (1990) summarized some of the ways that fifth and sixth graders reported "flow experiences:"

> One after the other, these children described what they enjoyed most about playing the piano, or swimming, or acting in the school plays. One said that while doing these things,

"I can forget my problems." Another said, "I can keep the things that bother me out of my mind" and so on. In class, they claimed, they could seldom achieve such concentration.

(p. 130)

During their time at school, students reported a cycle of experiences in which their concentration wandered repeatedly. Researchers concluded that while flow experiences occurred in academic settings, possibilities for immersion depended on the nature of the academic task and the level of support from teachers. Teachers who "intuitively know that the best way to achieve their goals is to enlist students' interest on their side and who do this by being sensitive to students' goals and interests" have the best chance of encouraging such immersion (p. 137).

They empower students to take control of their learning; they provide clear feedback to the students' efforts without making them self-conscious. They help students concentrate and get immersed in the symbolic world of the subject matter.

(p. 137)

To illustrate these dynamics, we share portions of a case study conducted with a student in a recent research report (Strahan, Poteat, Potts, Swords, & Wild, 2019). In this study, we observed lessons, gathered work samples, and interviewed eighth graders to describe their perspectives on developmental changes they were experiencing and on their teachers' efforts to integrate social and emotional learning with language arts. We found that students' reading comprehension grew richer when they were encouraged to make personal connections and provided a range of choices for expressing their understanding. Michael's case study demonstrates how he developed an interest in role-play gaming and how this interest led him to more ambitious reading.

Keep Flow Theory in mind as you meet Michael and witness the contrast between the surface-level work he produced when not particularly interested and the things he developed when he was deeply engaged with a topic or activity.

In his interviews with researchers, Michael sometimes came across as a reserved, shy boy of few words. Other times, interviewers found Michael to be an engaging, enthusiastic conversationalist. Michael told us he enjoys playing video games, as well as reading science fiction, graphic novels, and comics. Like many of his classmates, Michael engaged with lessons when he was interested in the topic or the activity. He especially enjoyed a social studies project on the achievements of Roman ingenuity. He selected methods of warfare as his topic and talked in detail about weapons and uniforms, subjects he found fascinating.

When not so interested, he was rather passive. During lesson observations, researchers noted that he preferred to seat himself on the sidelines and rarely participated in discussion. On informal assessments, researchers observed that Michael read words in isolation at the independent and instructional levels up through a sixth-grade level despite his place in eighth grade.

For his novel project, Michael chose to make a book trailer. He created nine slides that he linked together with background music. For each slide, Michael imported a picture he found on the internet that related to the name of the character. For example, one of the photos he imported for Roger was Roger Daltry. For Penelope, he chose a Greek statue. The slides ran by quickly, and the entire presentation lasted 41 seconds. In a debriefing interview, Michael explained that he did not really like the book but wanted to portray the main characters.

In the weeks that followed the project presentations, researchers made several efforts to engage Michael in conversations about the novel. He was always polite when questioned, yet he rarely gave more than one-word answers or said, "I don't know." While admitting he enjoyed the drawings and the funny parts of the book, he stated that he would not remember much about it.

During the time period when students were completing the novel, Michael's language arts teacher noticed that he had created his own fantasy board game and invited some of his friends to play the game with him at lunchtime. Researchers sat down with him and asked him to show them how to play his game. He spread out a hand-drawn diagram of a fantasy world and opened a bag with five sets of elaborate game dice of four different colors, some with as many as 15 sides. Numbers ranged from 1 to 80, creating many possible combinations of numbers and colors.

> Interviewer: This game board is very detailed. What is it about this game you find so interesting?
>
> Michael: It is a fun activity. I've seen other board games. I like this because there are a lot of dice. You can have them in your hands. And then it's your decision, not like in a pre-made game or a video game, even though I like playing video games too. You get to do whatever you would like, okay, and then the dice determine what happens.
>
> Interviewer: So, if other people want to play this, how would it play out? Each person takes on a role, right?
>
> Michael: There are more possibilities in mind. If a player suggests something, then it might be possible. I am the one that everything has to come through.

To get a better sense of how the game works, we asked Michael to show us how to play. Michael assumed his role as Game Master and arranged the dice. He assigned the interviewer the role of a dwarf.

> Michael: I am putting you on the entrance to the Smoke Mountain. You are a simple swordsman with armor, and you are about to arrive at the main gate. There is a massive human convoy of merchants that arrives. Do you signal the gatekeeper to open the doors, or do you wait on the slavers?
>
> Interviewer: Oh, I want the doors open so I can get in there.
>
> Michael: [rolls the dice] The combined number is 15. Eighty would have been a high number. So, as soon as the doors open, one of the guards notices you are a dwarf and takes you prisoner. The prison is a dark stone hole with several slaves already there.
>
> Interviewer: I want to win them over, free some of them so we can even the odds.

> Michael: [rolls the dice] It is all good. You've got the numbers [total of 56.] You are gaining strength. You now have armor and food.
>
> Interviewer: So, we're now a small group and we move into the city [refers to the map]. We need a place to hide out.
>
> Michael: Well, another trader spots you and realizes that some of you don't look like traders. He calls the guards and you run into the ruins. Now you are in a dark place with who knows how many monsters. If you roll a high number, I will count that as a successful escape.

At this point, the interviewer asked to pause the game to talk more about the process.

> Interviewer: How do you keep up with all of these details? Do you have a picture in your head or keep a running record?
>
> Michael: I don't know. I can do it—I just do it.
>
> Interviewer: So, when you're playing with your friends, do they bring ideas to the game and add new stuff?
>
> Michael: If they say they encounter something, then we put it in the game. I don't tell them what could happen. For example, there are dragons in lots of places, but I don't tell them that. I want them to be surprised.

This excerpt from Michael's case study shows the contrast between his conversations about his reading assignment and about his game. In game play mode, Michael demonstrated exceptional verbal creativity. He enjoyed the role of Game Master and readily took control of all aspects of the game. He gave directions and asked questions in rapid fashion, with no hesitation regarding the next event or outcome. Michael's intensity, enjoyment, and demeanor during game play was dramatically different from his persona during reading conversations with researchers.

We noticed that Michael introduced his game to several of his classmates. Soon a group of six were playing the game almost every day at lunchtime. One day, Michael surprised us by bringing in a *Dungeons and Dragons* game set. Michael asked if they could begin using that set instead of his hand-drawn game. Soon all six students were playing at lunch every day. Michael served as Game Master and read directions from the manual in a natural fashion that held players' attention. After we observed this scenario, we conducted a readability analysis on the game book as a reference point. Readability estimates ranged from tenth-grade to twelfth-grade level.

These illustrations from Michael's case study demonstrate the strength of engagement, or flow, when students are passionate about activities. In some lessons, Michael appeared to be a reluctant learner. In other lessons, like the social studies lessons on ancient Rome, he was much more active. On traditional reading tests, his performance indicated that he read below grade level. With the *Dungeons and Dragons* manual, he could deliver like a high school student.

Had we been able to read Michael's mind as he engaged with game play, we might have noted how his thoughts grew richer and deeper. The mental representations he formed as he created his own game and as he read the *Dungeons and Dragons* manual were elaborate and creative. Abstractions such as strategies and risk factors from decisions developed naturally. Emotions such as enjoyment of strange creatures and curiosity about possible worlds fueled this growing sophistication. At times, Michael became so engrossed in game play that he lost track of time.

This analysis of Michael's thinking illustrates many of the dynamics of intellectual and emotional development. The physical changes he experienced in his brain as he grew enhanced his capacity for executive function, enabling him to construct sophisticated representations of concepts he found interesting and of game play scenarios. Enhanced metacognition allowed him to channel his mental energies toward challenging new experiences. A growing passion for fantasy games led him to stretch his reading abilities, leading to deeper levels of reasoning. His teachers were able to create some curricular connections with his interests through reading options and writing assignments. Perhaps more importantly, by noticing his interests and talking with him about them, they showed they valued him and affirmed his sense of self.

Conclusions

Cognitive scientists remind us that adolescents are specially primed to learn from their own particular experiences during this developmental period. The powerful role that personal experience plays in their reasoning development means that there is tremendous variation within the general patterns we have described. Successful teachers draw from research on brain growth and learning processes to provide a foundation for understanding how students think and feel. They identify ways students make sense of new information and adjust instruction accordingly, for both groups and individuals. Engaging lesson activities integrate personal learning experiences with content concepts. As suggested in our Framework for Teaching Well, these efforts to understand and support developmental changes strengthen positive relationships and guide understanding, while nurturing trust and collaboration.

In this chapter, we have examined the role emotions play in the cognitive aspects of development, as well as the interplay among prior knowledge, instructional experiences, and context. In the next chapter, we extend this analysis to focus more specifically on the social and personal aspects of development.

Activities for Understanding Students Better

As in past chapters, we end here with examples of classroom activities that you might use to apply and enhance the topics discussed in this chapter. Consider your individual students and their specific levels of development, modifying these as necessary.

Concept Maps
Concept maps have been useful tools for teachers for many years. Popularized by the work of David Ausubel and other educational psychologists in the 1960s, the strategy builds on the notion of using visual diagrams to represent ideas, an instinct that has probably been with us for

centuries. In the preface to his book *Educational Psychology: A Cognitive View*, Ausubel wrote, "If [he] had to reduce all of educational psychology to just one principle, [he] would say this: The most important single factor influencing learning is what the learner already knows. Ascertain this and teach him accordingly" (Ausubel, 1968, p. vi).

In its simplest form, a concept map is a graphic organizer that enables a student to create a representation of key terms and relationships among them. A concept map often features ideas and information as boxes or circles connected by lines or arrows. Teachers use concept maps as both a diagnostic tool and instructional strategy.

Basic directions are

1. Identify important words and ideas related to the topic.
2. Arrange terms and ideas on paper in a way that reflects the relationships among them.

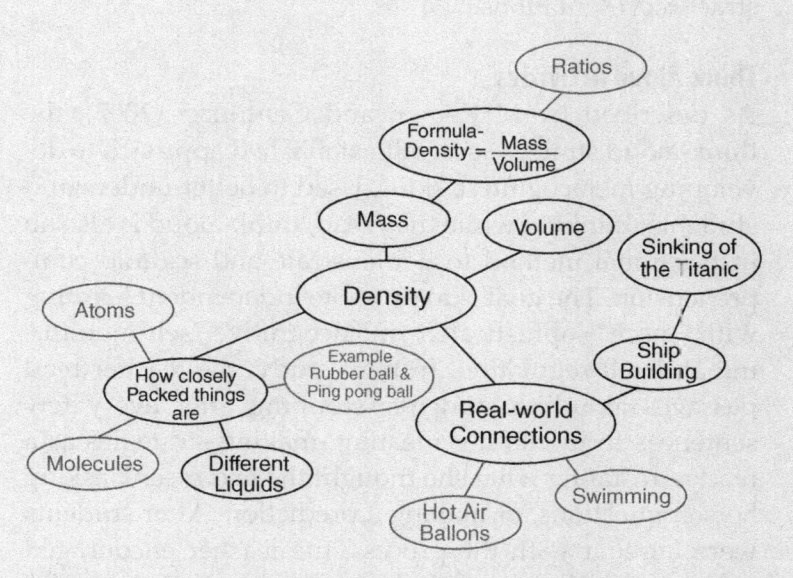

Figure 3.3 Gabrielle's concept map of concepts related to density (student artwork)

3. Add illustrations or other artwork to provide visual references for terms and ideas.

Here is a sample from a lesson on density described earlier in this chapter:

When we study Gabrielle's concept map, we can see that she connected the concept "density" to three related aspects: the formula relating density to mass and volume, how closely packed things are, and real-world connections. She began her map with these three circles and examples around them. With that first map, we see that she can identify a range of terms related to the concept and think of relationships among them. As she learned more about density, she added more specific sub-concepts. Her map shows us how the connections she made grew more detailed. If we asked her to explain some of her expanded connections, like swimming or hot air balloons, we might find that she is thinking at a deeper level with more abstract representations.

Think-Aloud Activities

As described by McKeown and Gentilucci (2007), the think-aloud strategy is a well-established approach to developing metacognitive skills. Used to better understand students' thinking while they read, think-aloud is also an instructional method to demonstrate and scaffold comprehension. The goal is to promote independent learning with more sophisticated metacognitive self-monitoring and self-regulation. In their study, the teacher read passages aloud to students, stopping after every few sentences to model her meaning-making strategies as a reader, restating what she thought the text meant, asking herself questions, or making a prediction. After students were familiar with the process, the teacher encouraged students to talk about "what was going on in their heads" (p. 141).

We have found the think-aloud strategy to be a powerful tool for learning more about how to think about any academic content. The general procedure is simple.

- The teacher models how he or she makes sense of a text passage or problem-solving task.
- Students then practice thinking aloud as they work with a partner or in small groups.
- The teacher extends the think-aloud process with journal assignments.

When individuals struggle to understand a new concept, teachers can use the think-aloud strategy as a vehicle for interventions, conducting one-to-one sessions in which they alternatively model their own thinking to guide comprehension and ask students to talk about their thoughts as they answer questions or solve problems.

Some teachers have extended the think-aloud approach to encourage students to reflect on their emotions. Adolescent literature now represents multiple content areas and can be enjoyed in varied genres—novels, poems, play scripts, song lyrics, for example—and provides a wealth of opportunities for students to respond to questions like

- What do you think the character feels at this point?
- How does the author create those feelings?
- How does this passage make you feel?
- Have you ever experienced feelings like this?
- How did you handle those feelings?

Experience with these types of think-aloud discussions can become prompts for a wide range of writing assignments that can span multiple content areas; for example: journal entries, poems, song lyrics, short videos, blogs, speeches, or scripts for podcasts and TED talks. When

> thinking aloud becomes a recurring feature in a classroom, the teacher has a wealth of information about students' thoughts, and students are supported in trying out new modes of reasoning.

References

Ausubel, D.P. (1968). *Educational psychology. A Cognitive View*. New York, NY: Holt, Rinehart and Winston, Inc.

Bernadowski, C. (2016) "I Can't Evn Get Why She Would Make Me Rite in Her Class": Using Think-Alouds in Middle School Math for "At-Risk" Students. *Middle School Journal*, 47(4), 3–14. DOI: 10.1080/00940771.2016.1202654

Biggs, J., & Collis K.F. 1982. *Evaluating the Quality of Learning: The SOLO Taxonomy*. New York, NY: Academic.

Biggs, J., & Collis, K. (1989). Towards a Model Of School-Based Curriculum Development and Assessment Using The Solo Taxonomy. *Australian Journal of Education*, 33(2), 151–163.

Crone, E. (2017). *The Adolescent Brain: Changes in Learning, Decision-Making, and Social Relations*. New York, NY: Routledge.

Csikszentmihalyi, M., & Nakamura, J. (1989). The Dynamics of Intrinsic Motivation: A Study of Adolescents. *Research on Motivation in Education*, 3, 45–71.

Csikszentmihalyi, M. (1990). Literacy and Intrinsic Motivation. *Daedalus*, 119(2), 115–140.

Fisher, D., Frey, N., & Hattie, J. (2016). *Visible Learning for Literacy*. Thousand Oaks, CA: Corwin.

Fuhrmann, D., Knoll, L.J., & Blakemore, S.J. (2015) Adolescence as a Sensitive Period of Brain Development. *Trends in Cognitive Sciences*, 19(10), 558–566.

Hattie, J. (2009). *Visible Learning: A Synthesis of Over 800 Meta-analyses Related to Achievement*. New York, NY: Routledge.

Hattie, J., & Yates, G. (2014). *Visible Learning and the Science of How We learn*. Oxon: Routledge.

Immordino-Yang, M.H. (2016). *Emotions, Learning and the Brain: Exploring the Educational Implications of Affective Neuroscience*. New York, NY: W. W. Norton and Company.

Kahneman, D. (2011). *Thinking fast and Slow*. New York, NY: Farrar, Straus, and Giroux.

McKeown, R.G., & Gentilucci, J.L. (2007). Think-Aloud Strategy: Metacognitive Development and Monitoring Comprehension in the Middle School Second-Language Classroom. *Journal of Adolescent and Adult Literacy*, 51(2), 136–147.

Nagaoka, J., Farrington, C.A., Ehrlich, S.B., & Heath, R.D. (2015). *Foundations for Young Adult Success: A Developmental Framework*. Chicago, IL: The University of Chicago Consortium on Chicago School Research.

National Academies of Sciences, Engineering, and Medicine. (2019). *The Promise of Adolescence: Realizing Opportunity for All Youth*. Washington, DC: The National Academies Press. https://doi.org/10.17226/25388

Noyce, P. (2017). *Mosquitoes Don't Bite Me*. Boston, MA: Tumblehome Learning, Inc.

Pinker, S. (1997). *How the Mind Works*. New York, NY: Penguin Books.

Strahan, D., Poteat, B., Alyssa Potts, A., Swords, H., & Wild, E. (2019). Integrating Social and Emotional Learning with Language Arts: Responses from Students. Paper presented at the Association for Middle Level Education, Nashville, TN, November.

Voight, C. (1986). *Izzy, Willy-Nilly*. New York, NY: Atheneum.

Willingham, D.T. (2009). *The Reading Mind: A Cognitive Approach to Understanding How the Mind Reads*. San Francisco, CA: Jossey-Bass.

4

Reflecting and Identifying
Patterns of Personal Development

In the previous chapters, we emphasized how the dramatic development that occurs during adolescence creates opportunities for students to grow stronger and to think in new ways. Physical changes transform bodies and minds toward adulthood, enabling accomplishments not possible in childhood. These changes also enable more sophisticated perceptions of self and others.

To put these changes into perspective, we often encourage participants in professional development sessions and university courses to think about themselves during their adolescent years. Although our experiences vary considerably, we find we all share the memories of good times and stressful moments. One of our favorite activities is to ask folks to take a quick trip down memory lane, which we invite you to do now as well. Please take a few minutes and answer the following questions from this specific year during your own adolescence:

1. What year was it when you were in the grade you now teach?
2. What were some of the songs you liked to hear?
3. What was happening in the wider world?
4. Who were some of your teachers?
5. Who were some of your friends?

DOI: 10.4324/9781003296614-4

Reflecting and Identifying ◆ 109

6. What did you do after school and on weekends?
7. What did you learn to do for the first time?
8. What are some of the words you might have used to describe yourself then?

Jeanneine remembers:

I recall the British Invasion, miniskirts, and especially those white patent leather go-go boots! London fashion was all the rage then—every girl wanted to dress like the magazine photos, including me, though that was not in my family's limited budget. I dreamed of those shiny white boots for months and months (not sure why, I have to admit now), but I was destined to just admire them on the feet of other girls. I accepted that readily, however, as I grew up in a rural community with a K-8 school where no one had many luxuries, but none of us ever felt the pinch. Ringo Starr was my love, and my childhood was definitely happy, though I was teased a lot for being the tallest girl in the seventh and eighth grades—and I mean the entire grade, not just my classroom, so I was pretty self-conscious. (Some of that happened in the form of Slam Books, an awful concept now that I think about it.) That was embarrassing, but I got over it in high school when the boys finally shot past me in height. My best friend then had always been my best friend and still is today, and she covered for me a lot when I stumbled into things I did not understand, especially about body changes, which, by the way, happened way later then than now, it seems.

Dave recalls:

I think back to the 1960s when the Beatles first burst on the music scene, Ed Sullivan was on television, and the Viet Nam war was heating up. Moving from a small elementary school to a big junior high was a challenge. Sports became more competitive and my dreams of playing high school basketball collided with reality. Having a paper route provided responsibility and extra money to spend on collecting coins and buying baseball cards. Thoughts and questions like "I'm not sure where I fit in." "Will

> *I ever grow tall?" and "Will Linda ever go to the movies with me?" were frequent worries of mine. High school loomed large and seemed frightening to me. Transitions, lots of changes.*

And Madison adds:

> *I remember the mid-2000s ... and honestly, things were just a little different than Dave and Jeanneine experienced. Due to mandated school uniforms, we expressed our personalities and identities through shoes and accessories—hair ribbons, pocketbooks, and eyeshadow, oh, and for a short period of time, Silly Bandz. My best friend, Alexis, and I kept a notebook to pass back and forth in class (especially band class) with secrets and plans for the weekend. Cell phones were just becoming popular, so bathroom conversations always centered on which boy you spent your 100 monthly texts on ... Was it Nathan? Or Dillon? Or Dylan? No matter the occasion—classes at school, sporting events, school dances—I always worried about my appearance, specifically my hair, weight, and complexion. Very eager to impress boys, I spent hours finding the perfect outfit to wear to the school dance where we'd all gather to dance to "Crank That (Soulja Boy)" and the "Cha Slide." Weekends were spent at friends' houses, messaging boys, on AIM with shorthand texts such as "WRUD?" "NM U?" "NM Just chillin." "K. Cool." (That was it. That was typically the full extent of a flirty conversation with your crush.) Some weekends I would go with friends to Late Night Skate where we would jam to songs like "Fergalicious," "Beautiful Girls," "Lip Gloss," and "Bubbly," to name a few. Despite the fun, insecurity ran rampant in my adolescent mind. Was I pretty enough? Smart enough? Funny enough? Skinny enough—but not too skinny, womanly? These worries were always at the forefront of my thinking and dictated most decisions I made.*

When participants in our classes begin discussing their recollections from our trip down memory lane, we often learn that the adolescent years were happy for some, not so happy for others. Though separated in age by years and decades, participants still recognize recurring patterns of feelings. No matter when or where we went to school, most of us wondered whom we were becoming and what would become of us. We fixated on friendships, wanted to keep up with the latest, worried about what was right and wrong with the world, and how we might fit into it all.

These recurring issues characterize developmental transitions in almost every time period, from then to now. In this chapter, we explore various aspects of personal growth, including the development of a more resilient sense of self, which is based on a clear understanding of personal identity.

Developing a More Resilient Sense of Self

From their first moments of life, babies try to make sense of the world around them. Children immediately learn to interpret sensory information to recognize people and objects. As they develop language, they begin to construct a sense of self by internalizing the verbal and non-verbal messages they receive.

> You are a sweet little girl.
> You are getting to be a big boy.
> Look how well you are standing up.
> You have a great smile.

Early notions of identity form in relationship to family and immediate surroundings. Children learn they have a place in a social system. They learn their names and define themselves as daughters or sons, brothers or sisters, grandchildren.

Through childhood and into adolescence, identity becomes increasingly defined. "Who am I?" and "How do I relate to others?" become pressing questions. In their analysis of developmental assets essential to well-being, Benson, Leffert, Scales, and Blyth (1998) identified four connected dimensions of positive identity development:

- *Personal power*—Young person feels he or she has control over "things that happen to me."
- *Self-esteem*—Young person reports having high self-esteem.
- *Sense of purpose*—Young person reports, "My life has a purpose."

♦ *Positive view of personal future*—Young person is optimistic about her or his personal future.

(p. 9)

A helpful framework for conceptualizing positive identity development is the construct of resilience. Adults have long wondered why some children experience adverse conditions and yet develop into strong and healthy adults. Over the years, researchers have examined ways children cope with traumatic experiences and how environmental factors influence their resiliency. Early hypotheses focused on innate aspects of personality and character, which suggested that some children were born with a capacity for resilience. More recently, we have begun to understand resiliency in a more interactive and contextual fashion. To clarify, Masten, Best, and Garmezy (1990) defined resilience as "a process of, or capacity for, or the outcome of successful adaptation despite challenging and threatening circumstances" (p. 459).

"I am poem" by Faye A. (Figure 4.1) expresses a powerful declaration of resilience. Her assertions that "Though you may not know me, my labels do not define me" and "I am me and only me" remind us that 13-year-olds can develop a clear, strong sense of self-efficacy.

To understand better how adolescents develop a more resilient sense of self, it is essential to consider resilience from this process-oriented perspective, situating resilience as the interactions of individuals with the people around them to negotiate negative life experiences. Wang, Zhang, and Zimmerman (2015) emphasized a strength-based orientation to resilience. In contrast to "deficit" and "problem-oriented" approaches, which focus on risk factors and vulnerabilities, a strength-based approach focuses on "promotive" factors that help adolescents "overcome adversity and achieve healthy development" (p. 356). Two promotive factors are especially important:

♦ Assets that refer to positive intrapersonal factors, such as perceived competence, coping skills, and self-efficacy.
♦ Resources that include parental support, adult mentoring, and youth programming.

(p. 356)

Reflecting and Identifying ◆ 113

I Am Poem
By Faye A., Grade 7

I Am

I am Faye

I am myself and only myself

Not the mask that covers my soul

Not the family I was born into

Not my culture, beliefs, or religion

Not my marks or IQ

I am who I choose to be

I am not defined by labels

The words girl, weak, ugly, and short are written all over me

Though no matter how hard I try to wash away the ink stains

They will never disappear

But that should not matter

For the ink is not visible to anyone who looks past it

What they see will be my true identity

Though you may not know me

My labels do not define me

It may take some time for you to see

But beneath this mask

I am me and only me

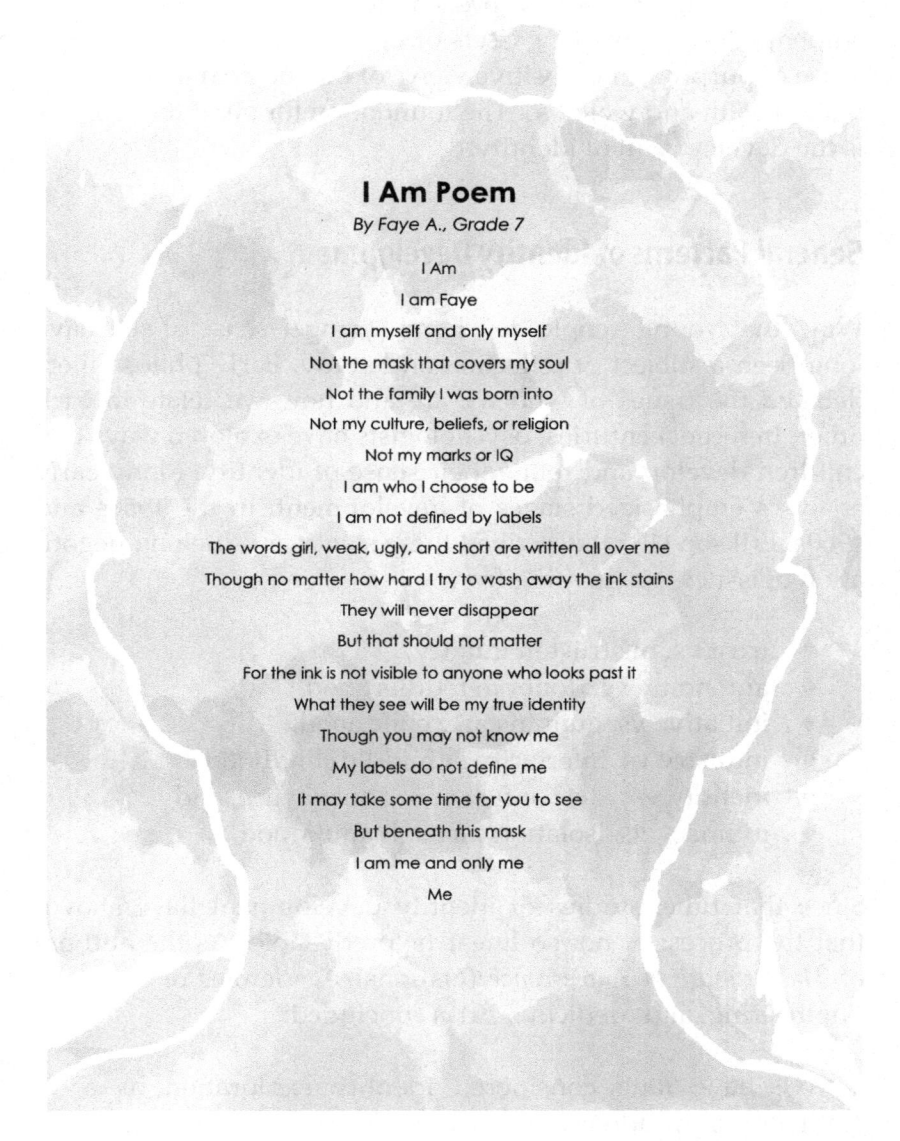

Me

Figure 4.1 "I am poem" by Faye A. Reproduced with permission from the Association for Middle Level Education. All rights reserved

This strength-based approach helps us understand how students develop the key assets of personal power, self-esteem, sense of purpose, and positive views of the future that are essential to health and wellness. The foundation for all of these assets is the development of identity.

General Patterns of Identity Development

Ways that young people develop a stronger sense of self have long been a subject of reflection and study. Early philosophers debated the issues of who we are and how we relate to each other. In recent centuries, psychologists have explored ways that children develop and refine their sense of identity. Many early analyses emphasized stages of development. In the 1950s and 1960s, Erikson (1959) described these stages as a lifelong negotiation of issues, progressing from

- trust vs. mistrust in infancy,
- autonomy vs. doubt in toddlerhood,
- initiative vs. guilt in early childhood,
- industry vs. inferiority in middle childhood,
- identity vs. role confusion in adolescence, and
- intimacy vs. isolation through adulthood.

Since that time, studies of identity development have shown that the process is not so linear or predictable. As the authors of *The Promise of Adolescence* (National Academies of Sciences, Engineering, and Medicine, 2019) concluded:

> We have long considered identity exploration as a hallmark of adolescence. An adolescent's identity is an emerging reflection of his or her values, beliefs, and aspirations, and it can be constructed and reconstructed over time and experience. Multiple factors—family, culture, peers, media—shape identity development, but young people are also active agents in the process.
> (p. 50)

The authors' review of the research describes identity development as an exploratory, interactive, and negotiated process. Growing powers of reasoning during adolescence enable new ways of thinking about self and others, as well as thinking about thinking itself. Making sense of who they are "requires adolescents to integrate multiple perspectives and experiences across contexts and also to deepen their ability to make sense of complex and abstract phenomena" (p. 44). Although a young adolescent may develop multiple "abstractions" of self, these growing images tend to be fragmented and sometimes even contradictory (p. 45).

Teachers who observe students carefully notice these dynamics. Students who are outgoing and friendly in one class may be withdrawn in another. A girl who seems timid in small group activities may be loud and boisterous at lunchtime. A boy who is confident on the basketball court may wilt under the pressure of a reading assessment. These contradictions illustrate ways that students enrich and extend their views of themselves.

Although each adolescent experiences these dynamics differently, researchers have identified distinct patterns:

- Self-concept first emerges in general terms. Children see themselves as good girls or good boys, boys who like trucks or girls who like sports. They internalize messages from family: "I am a Kentucky fan like my father." "My mother tells me I am a good helper."
- Over time, children expand their views of themselves. They become more aware of things about themselves that they like and, perhaps, things about themselves they wish they could change.
- In early adolescence, young teens' views of themselves grow more differentiated. Students begin to see themselves in varied ways across social and relational situations, revealing some aspects of self with family and other aspects with friends.
- As a result, students often explore different identities, think about themselves in reference to peers and media, and choose to identify with peers with whom they feel they belong.

Teachers frequently observe students trying on different identities. They may experiment with different hairstyles for a time, then try different hair colors, and then decide to take on a more natural persona. They might dress in athletic gear for a time, then shift to a hunter/camouflage style. High school students who once tried hard to keep up with the most popular fashions may begin to dress in ways that set themselves apart from the prevailing norms.

Regardless of the ways in which they express themselves outwardly, a school's influence on identity is understood, with this context playing a major contributory role in an adolescent's development. An analysis of 111 studies on a school's impact on identity development clearly supports this thought, and further indicates that "schools and teachers are often unaware of the many different ways in which they may significantly impact adolescents' identity development" (Verhoeven, Poorthuis, & Volman, 2018, p. 36). Concentrating primarily on personal and social identity, the researchers systematically examined selected studies and concluded that, across studies, the classroom context and the teacher's control of it can hinder or enhance identity development in students. One of these studies, for instance (Horn, 2008), found that mathematics teachers who required students to work individually contributed to some students' innate belief that their abilities were capped. When they could no longer understand how to push ahead, students began to perceive that they were simply not good in the subject. This was in direct opposition to classrooms where the teacher and students worked on problems collaboratively; those environments found students of varying abilities working together with the teacher to uncover common solutions, thus moving all students to an unbounded measure of success. In this way, teachers' unintentional expectations directly contributed to the identity development of their students in terms of scholarship.

Likewise, the same could perhaps be said of students who enter the classroom with notoriety for certain behaviors that are negative or positive—as teachers, we may overlook a student's own efforts to mitigate those negative reputations as an adolescent matures and begins to project him or herself into a different persona. All of this can dramatically affect a student's self-image and self-talk. "Yet, whether the perceived teacher expectations that are reported represent truth, imagination, or both, the studies do suggest that adolescents' self-understandings are informed by their perceptions of their teachers' expectations" (Verhoeven et al., 2018, p. 46). Further, this might manifest itself in the classroom by subtle teacher-initiated cues such as these: not recognizing a raised hand, implicitly communicating low expectations for academics or behavior, seating a student in a certain position in the classroom, assigning status within an ability group such as Honors and AP courses, or either shunning or promoting roles given students' ethnic/racial groups (Verhoeven et al., 2018). Finally, the authors posit that introducing adolescents to new experiences and situations (e.g., field trips, summer programs, explorative opportunities) can "invite them to adopt new interests, to identify undiscovered talents, and to try out new identity positions" (p. 49), including on-site and hands-on pursuits that accompany a measure of risk-taking and self-reflection. All told, incorporating supportive, collaborative, explorative learning experiences into the classroom curriculum can enhance every adolescent's healthy growth and development in many ways, with identity and self-perceptions chief among them.

Conscientious, proactive support is especially important when students may risk any form of stereotyping, experiencing social structures that marginalize or privilege people at the intersections of race, class, gender, sexual orientation, gender expression, and ability. For students labeled with exceptionalities, the processes of exploration and negotiation of identity are heavily influenced by curricular and pedagogical choices in schools (Dunn & Burcaw, 2013). Adolescents with disabilities negotiate a host of thoughts about, and experiences with, their impairment and the meaning of that impairment to their broader sense of who they are. This negotiation is influenced by, and developed alongside, intersectional identities like race that shape understandings of people as their whole selves (Mueller, 2021). Understanding more about the inner workings of identity development may help us develop the proactive systems of support necessary to nurture positive perceptions of self in all students.

Identity Development as a Negotiated Process

As we emphasized in the previous chapters, rapid development of the structure and function of the brain enables thinking that is more sophisticated. Adolescents constantly try to make sense of the information that bombards them. Immersed in messages from parents, teachers, peers, and the media, they sort and interpret, respond and reflect. Many of the messages prompt emotional responses, sometimes intensely so, as puberty brings new ways of thinking and feeling. As reminded, young people are not passive recipients of these messages. Even when they find them confusing or troubling, adolescents are actively engaged in sense-making. They try on new identities, try out new behaviors, make decisions about who they are and whom they want to become (National Academies of Sciences, Engineering, and Medicine, 2019).

Crone (2017) emphasized the importance of introspection and self-awareness in developing identity, an important dimension of which is adolescents thinking about how other people think about them. She noted that this heightened self-awareness sometimes triggers egocentricity when "introspection can sometimes cause them to become completely absorbed by their thoughts about themselves" (p. 102). She described two important ways egocentricity manifests itself. When adolescents become especially self-absorbed, they develop a sense of "imaginary audience," convinced that everyone is watching them and making judgments about them. A second way is the "personal fable," in which they are sure that their personal experiences are unique. "Scientists believe the personal fable may be a means of boosting adolescents' self-confidence, as it gives them a feeling they are unique. However, the personal fable can be deceiving when leading them to the feeling of invulnerability" (p. 102). Crone concluded that as introspection grows more intense, growing powers of reasoning enable stronger perspective-taking.

> Before children enter adolescence, they have trouble empathizing with other people's thoughts and feelings. But once they have entered adolescence, they learn to empathize with the feelings and thoughts of others and even

to take a third person's perspective. This means that they understand that the feelings and thoughts of Person A influence the feelings and thoughts of Person B.

(p. 117)

In recent years, the pervasiveness of social media has complicated this sense-making process. Negotiating identity when bombarded by media images creates a level of intensity beyond that of previous generations. Gardner and Davis (2013) analyzed longitudinal studies, interviewed more than 150 young people, conducted focus groups with adults who work with youth in a variety of capacities, and interviewed 40 teachers. They scrutinized visual artworks and writing samples gathered over 20 years. They concluded that today's youth could be characterized as an "App Generation."

> It's our argument that young people growing up in our time are not only immersed in apps: they come to think of the world as an ensemble of apps, to see their lives as a string of ordered apps, or perhaps in many cases, a single extended, cradle-to-grave app.
>
> (p. 7)

Further, today's youth communicate in ways different from their pre-digital counterparts: internet-enabled cell phones, tablets, and laptops. This near-constant flow of information makes social interactions highly public. Participation in events, invitations to parties, performance on exams—all these can become matters of public record with a few keystrokes.

Finally, Gardner and Davis found that growing up in the App Generation creates unique challenges to the negotiation of identity. They concluded that the identities of young people are increasingly packaged.

> That is, they are developed and put forth so that they can convey a certain desirable, indeed interminably upbeat, image of the person in question... On the positive side, there is also a broadening of acceptable identities (it's

okay to be a geek; it's okay to be gay). Overall, life in an app-suffused society yields not only many small features of a person's identity but also pushes toward an overall packaged sense of self.

(p. 60)

Anderson and Jiang (2018) reported data from the Pew Research Center (2019) indicating that in just one year, the percentage of internet usage among adolescents grew from 78% in 2013 to 97% in 2014. Ninety-three percent of teens aged 13 and 14 own a smartphone, 86% have a gaming console, and 88% have a computer. While middle and upper income families have higher levels of computer access, youth across all income categories reported high levels of cell phone access. By 2018, 95% of US teenagers had access to a smartphone at home, and 45% claimed to be online "almost constantly" (Turner, Hicks, & Zucker, 2019, p. 304).

Adolescents face several challenges in this online environment. Stevens (2017) reported studies showing that although social media can provide a sense of connection, posts may exaggerate the feelings of others and make teens feel less successful in comparison. One study at Temple University with 32 teenagers monitored brain responses during social media engagement. Participants viewed images on social media that had been assigned random numbers of likes by researchers. Brain scans showed participants usually skipped over images with few likes and spent more time viewing photos that had been assigned many likes. The reward pathways in the brain (the area known as the *nucleus accumbens*) were most active when participants viewed pictures of themselves with many likes assigned. Likes functioned as powerful social cues.

In similar studies, photos showing risky behaviors, such as smoking or drinking, often reduced activity in the portion of the brain responsible for cognitive control, suggesting that social media might encourage teens to let down their guard with some risky behaviors, which can provide further insights into the spontaneous decision-making example found in Chapter 3. When researchers altered social media posts to increase the number of likes, response times increased accordingly. This was especially the case when posts featured other adolescents drinking. "Social media users see only highlights from the party. These are the posts that others like. People rarely, however, post pictures of their hangovers, poor grades or drinking-related injuries and accidents," Stevens noted (p. 2).

The online social world, other forms of media, classroom interactions, peer influence, parenting styles, new ways of thinking and feeling—adolescents actively engage in sense-making by trying out new behaviors and identities based on many factors. In this sometimes chaotic, mediated environment, however, they often struggle to establish a consistent, confident sense of self. As they work to find logic in simultaneous messages, some of the most pressing issues grow especially complicated.

One strategy that has proven successful for guiding introspection and self-awareness within a portion of those complicated issues is Figurative Transformation, a framework that instructs students to depict their academic and personal transformations in a metaphorical way (DePaul University, 2022). Madison has found that this strategy encourages students to highlight their self-analysis regarding learning and personal growth. Consider her illustration as you picture this in your own classroom:

Figurative Transformation Activity

What is it and when should I use it? *This activity asks your students to articulate creatively how they have changed throughout the term. It works well at the end of the academic quarter or semester, or other natural junctures.*

  Why would I use it? *This opportunity highlights self-development and personal growth by having your students articulate goals and describe how your course prepares them for future educational and professional experiences. It also inspires creative thinking and curriculum engagement.*

  What exactly do I do? *Ask your students to imagine themselves and their transformation in the course through an extended metaphor.*

For example, you might ask students to imagine themselves as a superhero, and then describe (in words or in a drawing):

- *The story of their transformation into a superhero (an account of how they changed in the course)*
- *The superpowers they gained (strengths and abilities they have gained in the course)*
- *Their kryptonite (challenges yet to overcome, areas for improvement)*

Here's how I used this:
The students in my freshman English class had come to the end of their first quarter in high school, a quarter that ended in their Hero's Journey unit. To assess students' understanding of the unit content, as well as see how students are adjusting to high school, I closed the unit through a Figurative Transformation product creation rather than a more traditional exam or essay assignment.

I began by asking students to visualize their eighth-grade self, including their strengths and shortcomings. I then prompted them to make a list of their personal, academic, and social qualities from that past academic grade level. After making that list, they added all the ways they had grown since leaving middle school, including

- *What have you learned about yourself personally, academically, and relationally?*
- *How have you matured?*
- *What skills can you perform better now than before?*

We then distributed markers, magazines, construction paper, scissors, and glue, and I announced, "Okay, now for your unit assessment." After experiencing a big unit heavy with reading and writing, they gave me puzzled looks and I went on, "Today, you are going to show me not only your personal transformation but also who you are academically. Use your understanding of figurative language, character traits, and metacognition. Illustrate your personal journey from middle school to high school and how you have grown into a stronger, more intelligent, and more creative student since the close of your eighth-grade year. If you don't love drawing, but prefer creating a short film, or even writing a short story, you have free rein when it comes to what you create, but it must be detailed and figurative. You need to build a fictional 'you.'"

Students struggled at first. Some asked to just take a test or write an essay, but I encouraged them to have fun and really spend time thinking about their growth and evolvement. Students started drawing, brainstorming, sharing ideas, and creating, and the classroom quickly grew silent.

This activity became, foremost, a great way for students to dig inside themselves for the ninth graders they had become: Whom am I growing into? What am I confident about now? What sort of friend am I becoming? What's ahead for me to keep working on? It also emphasized academic elements such as figurative language, symbolism, characterization, and conflict, and I've ended up using this assignment several times. Even though the example here is for ELA, I think you can easily modify it for other content areas as well. It continues to provide me with a terrific way to incorporate social and emotional learning and conversation into my classroom while assessing an academic unit and showcasing metacognition. Encouraging my students to reflect on their evolution and to depict it through this assignment nurtures creativity, introspection, reflection, and critical thinking in a highly engaging way.

The Figurative Transformation strategy demonstrates one way to teach explicitly some aspects of the sophisticated thinking many students find challenging. Supporting introspection and self-awareness is especially important as adolescents negotiate their identities.

Negotiating Ethnic-Racial and Gender Identity

Two of the biggest aspects of the "Who am I?" question are ethnic-racial and gender identities. While these two questions prompt different challenges, they occur at the same time developmentally and intertwine in the sense-making process.

In Chapter 2, Jaleisha shared her experiences working with Kayla, a seventh grader for whom early maturation brought challenges as a young African American adolescent. As her teacher and an African American herself, Jaleisha fully understood Kayla's situation. Struggling with how to be a 12-year-old in a woman's body made Kayla feel out-of-sync with classmates and uncertain as to how to interact with adults. Her questions of "how to be a woman" and "how to be African American" became a tangle for her, and Jaleisha was able to use her position as a classroom teacher to influence Kayla's identity development positively. In this section of the chapter, we will explore some of the research related to both issues.

As our nation's population grows increasingly diverse, researchers have identified ethnic-racial identity (ERI) as a critical factor in health, wellness, and achievement. In their summary of the broad-based, interdisciplinary research of the Ethnic and Racial Identity in the 21st Century Study Group, Umaña-Taylor and her colleagues (2014) define ERI as a "multidimensional, psychological construct that reflects the beliefs and attitudes that individuals have about their ethnic-racial group memberships, as well as the processes by which these beliefs and attitudes develop over time" (p. 23). As an integrative construct, ERI encompasses students' beliefs about their group and how their ethnicity becomes a central aspect of their self-definition.

The ERI study group described ways that ERI begins to form as children learn to identify and categorize people with ethnic and racial labels. As they approach adolescence, young people form more specific conceptualizations as they try to make sense of the external messages related to the social constructs of race and ethnicity. They begin to see how race and ethnicity impact people's lives—and their own—and they internalize values from significant others. They recognize how life experiences vary from one racial and ethnic group to another. In later adolescence, more sophisticated perspective-taking skills enable strong considerations of what ERI means to them, and not just what it means to their families and peers.

Life experiences—such as encounters with peers from other racial and ethnic groups, media messages, moments of discrimination, and inquiries into the history of their families and their ethnicity, and schooling—shape this process of self-definition. Huang and Stormshak (2011) conducted a longitudinal study with diverse groups of students from sixth to ninth grades. They found that students experienced a process of exploring issues and affirming identities, a process previously noted (Verhoeven et al., 2018). For most students, ERI grew stronger and more certain with reinforcement from family and peers.

The extent to which students form positive ethnic identities is a critical factor in their development. Rivas-Drake et al. (2014) reported a meta-analysis based on 46 studies of ethnic identity and psychosocial, academic, and health risk outcomes among minority youth from four major US ethnic-racial groups (African American, Latinx, Asian American, and Native American). Findings demonstrated that positive ethnic-racial affect was associated with positive social functioning, self-esteem, and well-being, as well as academic achievement and academic attitudes. These correlations underscore the role of positive ethnic-racial affect in developing internal assets that foster resilience.

To learn more about the ways adolescents develop those assets, Rivas-Drake and Umaña-Taylor (2019) examined the development of ethnic identity and the influence of context. Weaving together a wide range of interviews with young people, they identified five primary influences: family, peers, school, community, and media.

Beginning in early childhood, family experiences create the foundation for the development of ethnic identity. Researchers found that some families regularly celebrate their ethnic identity, some wrestle with related issues, and some try to avoid or ignore issues. Adolescents from families who made conscious efforts to help children learn about their heritage demonstrated higher levels of psychological well-being, social competence, and school success. Families who engaged in this process of "cultural socialization" often connected awareness at home with extended family experiences (p. 77).

As noted earlier, as students grow into upper elementary, middle, and high school, schools become important settings.

> A great deal of ethnic-racial socialization occurs in school halls, cafeterias, and classrooms in adolescence, and on college campuses in later years. Everywhere one turns, it

> seems there is evidence of how race and ethnicity shape the daily experience of youth in school: whom they learn with, whom they sit with at lunch, and whom they hang out with. It makes a lot of sense that youth turn to each other to pick up signals about what is expected when it comes to racial and ethnic identity.
>
> (p. 82)

School settings provide daily opportunities for students to explore who they are and where they belong. Astute teachers regularly observe ways that students cluster together along ethnic-racial lines whenever they have a chance to congregate. "Members of each 'flock' significantly influenced each other's subjective, psychological sense of identity, too. In other words, youths' views *evolved* as a function of their friendship" (p. 83).

In school settings, peer norms become especially influential. Teachers notice that students share norms of language, style and dress. At a deeper level, peer dynamics impact ways of viewing self and others—how to act, talk, and engage—whether to conform to identity ideals and social hierarchies. In interviews with researchers, participants emphasized the importance of peer relationships.

> Friends, simply put, matter a great deal in the ethnic-racial identity process among adolescents, just as they do for myriad issues during this period of life. This is not surprising, given their increasingly greater reliance on peers, more generally, as harbingers of what is good, acceptable, and desirable in a particular social and cultural context, such as school ... Yet peers not only serve as models of what particular ethnic-racial identities can look and sound like in school, but they also regulate each other to maintain conformity to particular identity ideals and social hierarchies.
>
> (p. 84)

Some of the experiences participants shared in their interviews revealed the power of seemingly casual incidents in hallways or at lunch. Teachers are familiar with these types of exchanges and the ways in which they can positively influence them. For example, a Latina student might overhear two students using stereotypical language, speaking just loudly enough that they know she will hear them. How she feels about those comments—and how she reacts—will influence her view of self as a Latina. If she internalizes a sense that she is somehow in a lower social group or does not belong in the dominant school culture, comments like these will shake her self-esteem and significantly affect her relationship with the school and those within it. However, if she can talk about these experiences with someone she trusts who is willing to engage in this difficult conversation, she may recognize stereotypes for what they are; that, in turn, can lead her to realize that she is capable of processing and responding to injustices from those who have yet to unlearn the harmful effects of prejudices. This could then lead her to a more positive and confident personal identity.

Many teachers are familiar with the notion that some students resist traditional expectations for conformity to avoid accusations of "acting white." Rivas-Drake and Umaña-Taylor's (2019) analysis of research and interviews suggests that this perception by teachers oversimplifies the dynamics of peer socialization. For some students, avoiding accusations of acting white is more about solidarity with fellow minority students than a rejection of Whiteness.

> Considered in this light, an accusation of inauthenticity serves the same purpose when it is levied by any group and references any other: Puerto Rican youth trying to be Asian, White youth wanting to be Black, and so on ... The point is that adolescents are vigilant about one another's dispositions and behaviors, and they construct mutually negotiated boundaries of an authentic group membership.
> (p. 86)

Researchers further emphasized the critical role teachers and administrators play in the development of ethnic identity:

> As they do with parents and peers, youth are observing and making sense of what adults at school do (or ignore)

> and say (or are silent about) with regard to race. When White youth attend an all-White school where race is never addressed explicitly, they too are learning about race: they are learning how to not notice and talk about it, perhaps how to avoid it altogether.
> (Rivas-Drake & Umaña-Taylor, 2019, p. 88)

In the hallway scenario we described earlier, the presence of a perceptive teacher could influence the situation significantly. If a teacher heard the comments and did nothing, the girls who made the slanderous remark might interpret silence as compliance with their attitude. Whether the offending students are ignored, scolded, punished, or brought into a purposeful conversation about the harmful effects of marginalizing, the teacher sends powerful messages about what is and is not acceptable in society. If we are to create classrooms anchored in authentic caring, we must step forward courageously and assist our students in unlearning those harmful stereotyping behaviors, both conscious and unconscious. As we have emphasized throughout this book, relationships deeply matter.

Rivas-Drake and Umaña-Taylor stressed that the most influential teachers demonstrate this pervasive attitude of "authentic caring," showing they respect students as individuals, understand and embrace their cultural backgrounds, and address their strengths in lessons. "In short, it means that adults challenge themselves to combat implicit biases or stereotypes (positive and negative) they might have to ultimately convey that youth are worth their care" (p. 92).

Some of the biggest challenges teachers face when they support ethnic identity are policy issues. How students are disciplined, how they are grouped for classes, how grades are assigned—all of these policies and practices can enhance or diminish perceptions of ethnicity. By themselves, caring teachers may not be able to change policy. However, they can express their values, talk with colleagues, and speak out when given the opportunity.

> As youth receive multiple, sometimes conflicting messages within and across each of their everyday contexts,

> they necessarily make choices about what to internalize as they craft their own individual identities. Taking all the information together, it is hard to know what to conclude for oneself. It is overwhelming, no doubt, and young people need adults in their lives to help them to unpack, interpret, and process all of these messages… For individuals who would like nothing more than to build bridges across different ethnic-racial experiences, it is critical to plunge into potentially socially and politically tense situations, and to have so-called brave conversations from *steady*, not shaky, ground.
> (Rivas-Drake & Umaña-Taylor, 2019, p. 98)

General processes of identity development—exploring one's sense of self, interpreting messages from others, engaging in social comparisons—characterize the development of ethnic and racial identities, as well as gender and ability identities. Emblems of belonging and shared language signal membership for any kinship group—whether for informal friendships, athletic teams, or religious organizations. Essential to identity are connections with others with whom we can relate, others who value us and let us know we matter. As children grow into adolescence and explore who they are and how they relate to others, their views of themselves grow more differentiated.

Increasing attention to issues of gender in recent years makes the search for identity more visible and provides more opportunities for exploration than in years past. To this point, young people are disclosing same-sex identities at earlier ages. In the past decade, the average age at which LGBTQ youth report coming out to family and friends has fallen from the early 20s to around 14 (National Academies of Sciences, Engineering, and Medicine, 2019).

> The identity language and labels used among youth who are often placed under the umbrella of LGBTQ have continued to rapidly evolve. A growing number of LGBTQ youth say they have a nonbinary gender identity (i.e., neither male nor female) or sexual identity (e.g., pansexual, bisexual, queer). Indeed, young people appear to be

> leading a movement toward challenging existing categories and constructing new identities.
>
> (p. 50)

The authors note that while we might expect that health and wellness issues may be improving accordingly, data suggest that this is not so.

> Things do not appear to be getting "better" for LGBTQ youth: rather than diminishing, health disparities across multiple domains appear to be stable if not widening. This pattern may be explained by several factors, including greater visibility and associated stigma and victimization for LGBTQ youth, just at the developmental period during which youth engage in more peer regulation and bullying in general, especially regarding sexuality and gender.
>
> (p. 48)

As with all aspects of identity development, relationships with classmates and teachers are a key factor in promoting a healthy exploration of personal identity. The "authentic caring" that Rivas-Drake and Umaña-Taylor (2019) advocated for supporting ethnic-racial identity can make a big difference in all situations and can also apply to gender identity development—respecting students as individuals, understanding and embracing differences, addressing strengths in lessons. A narrative from one of our teacher colleagues illustrates these dynamics as they relate to gender identity in one student.

Classroom Narrative: Supporting Charlotte and Her Classmates

*Please note: The teacher who wrote this narrative has asked that her experience be shared anonymously to protect the confidentiality of students.

Working at my current school provides opportunities to work with a multitude of students from various backgrounds and life experiences. Sadly, a lot of the rural students who access our program face serious issues both in and out of the classroom. About 37% of our school's population accesses free and reduced lunch services and resides in a rural environment still facing a 3.5% unemployment rate and an opioid crisis where some 20% of high schoolers report experimenting with recreational prescription drugs. These factors hit a pinnacle of influence on the growing adolescent. A factor that is emerging in the middle school classroom often goes overlooked in most societal settings. Our current generation of students is becoming more and more aware of their own views of sexuality and gender, unlike anything experienced prior. This growing voice in our learning community is not new, but their comfortableness with being visible in the school environment is a great change from the past few decades.

Last school year, my eighth graders were immersed in our civil rights studies. At first, we started our studies as routinely as you might expect in a middle school social studies course right before lunch. A handful of students within this class had experienced injustices in their prior educational experiences and often asked "controversial" questions to promote alternative viewpoints. This voice is more than welcome, especially in their growing brains. One specific student, whom I will call Charlotte, inquired aloud if we could learn about other civil rights movements, such as the LGBTQ movement. Her request was echoed by multiple peers instantly. I was happy to oblige, so I immediately sought and received approval from administration and parents, and we began a different trajectory in our studies.

I began by introducing the students to different civil rights movements and concepts from United States history every day, expanding on each topic day-by-day. We covered the 100 years of LGBTQ history, female equality movements of the suffragettes and the modern-day women's march, and the current children's march against gun violence. We maneuvered the topics through multiple mediums, such as videos and primary source readings. We compared figures like Martin Luther King, Jr. to Malcolm X, but also discussed who Marsha P. Johnson was and the incredible courage she used to face targeted abuse by the NYPD in the 1960s. We watched documentaries about Cesar Chavez and heard first-person accounts of our peers' families caught in the United States' current border war. This was juxtaposed to our group reading of *To Kill a Mockingbird* (Lee, 1960).

Students were especially engaged as we read an account from an activist in the Children's March for Their Lives. Due to profiling and adultification, this young man had been targeted as a school shooter but instead was the victim of one. One of our eighth graders was so impassioned by this account that he decided to come out publicly to his entire class. The space we had created for open learning and conversations revealed that his peers were more trustworthy than he originally deemed.

What we were learning was obviously resonating. We had Charlotte to thank for advocating for this voice of the students in our learning space. I was reminded again that peer interactions can activate the reward centers of the brain as students engaged with these issues. My job was to listen and facilitate this learning in a safe environment with informed materials. By allowing them to access agency over their own learning, students could safely develop many different factors connected to their experiences, such as their Hispanic, Black, or LGBTQ identities.

Now I want to fast forward to our eighth-grade trip. We visit Atlanta for a cultural experience over a three-day period. We visit museums, attend shows at the Fox Theatre, and visit the local tourist watering holes like The World of Coca-Cola. This year we visited four different museums: The Martin Luther King Historical site, The

Breman Museum with a private Holocaust survivor presentation, The Center for Civil and Human Rights, and the Atlanta History Center.

We also viewed *Dear Evan Hansen* at the Fox Theatre. This experience quickly became our social justice curriculum in action. *Dear Evan Hansen* is a contemporary musical wrestling with issues of self-advocacy and the importance of being our authentic selves with others. Particularly for middle school students, *Dear Evan Hansen* humbly displays the negative side effects of someone trying to be someone they are not, living a different life on social media and with different peers. It displays the responsibility we have to be honest with others and with ourselves about how we truly feel. *Dear Evan Hansen* was the first musical many of our students had ever seen, especially a live performance in a prestigious theater. Students were taken aback by the narrative, portrayal of characters, and the palpable emotions felt amongst the audience sharing their viewing experience. We as educators placed a lot of importance on this specific event, asking students to "dress for the theater." At different parts of the show, we as a collective group shed tears and belted laughter as a community, shedding our interpersonal boundaries for two hours.

With the exception of the Breman Museum tour, which is led by a Holocaust survivor's progeny, we allowed our students to lead the student groups with an adult included in the mix. Driven by their interests, students had serious discussions about how they, too, would have been targeted if they were born in these different locations or time periods. They wrestled with their own identities, spanning from interracial parents, or Hungarian grandparents, to their impoverished roots. Relatedly, a handful of students were noticing that almost all revolving exhibits in these museums had begun to focus on LGBTQ rights and concerns all over the world. They studied life in Russia for the LGBTQ today or noticed how museum curators no longer hesitated to mention that a writer or inventor was gay and faced oppression for living as their authentic selves.

When we returned home, after a happenstance drive through the rainbow painted Mid-Town while lost in traffic, you could sense an evolution of spirit. Many of these students had already had the difficult conversation with their parents and peers about how they identify themselves and their sexual interests. Several LGBTQ teens openly dated at our school. They didn't want to remain invisible, though they perceived the expectation was to do so. Why? Because it *is* the expectation in a rural southern school that they remain quiet about their lifestyles in the school halls. With less than two months left in the school year, they wanted to leave a legacy of what they had learned.

The five students who wrestled deeply through our studies, and sobbed alongside all of their peers in *Dear Evan Hansen*, decided to start a Gay and Straight Alliance. Many of these students had long since been red-flagged by schools and medical professionals for issues concerning self-harm, depression, anxiety, and suicidal tendencies. This personal agency was critical to maintaining trust in our relationships with students and others who remained voiceless in our learning community. Students practiced social justice and democratic practices by electing councils, writing mission statements, and drafting core documents vital to the longevity of the group in our school. Students felt proud of their work, promoting it in the halls and during homeroom meetings. The founding members reached out to their younger peers, promoting their meeting as a safe space, growing their numbers over two meetings.

> By allowing an inclusive curriculum into our classrooms and supporting organizations driven by our students' needs and desires, we can counteract the startling statistics that are on the rise across our states and nation. Adolescents are at risk for so many different reasons, and when we exercise our ability to restore the voice of an entire demographic at this critical age, we can positively influence these students in ways education has far overlooked too long, thus changing trajectories over lifespans.

In this narrative, our teacher colleague embodies a stance of "authentic caring." She created a climate that nurtured high levels of respect and trust among students, and she engineered her classroom curriculum to allow for the development of personal identities, including those of marginalized LGBTQ students. She developed strong working relationships with them as individuals and as a group. She made it clear that differences were embraced and conversations would be authentic. She designed lessons that would enrich and extend these relationships as well as examine important issues in social studies. Consequently, students were empowered to support each other and take ownership of the curriculum.

Her narrative also illustrates ways caring teachers support the development of a more resilient sense of self. Her classroom became a place where students could explore identities, learn to interpret messages from others with greater sophistication, and engage in supportive social comparisons.

Conclusions

As we suggested at the beginning of this chapter with our "trip down memory lane" activity, most adults have vivid memories of adolescence. We remember that the people we became were different from the children we had been. Observing these changes as teachers can help us create stronger connections with our students.

From the perspective of positive youth development, adolescents negotiate physical changes, mental growth, and life experiences to achieve a more resilient sense of self. They make sense of the messages they receive and their encounters with the world to gain confident views of their identities. Learning experiences in school can accelerate these positive trajectories when teachers find ways to integrate the realities of day-to-day life with academic study.

Positive trajectories grow strongest when teachers provide the "authentic caring" that Rivas-Drake and Umaña-Taylor (2019) emphasized. The research we have reviewed and the narratives from our teacher colleagues demonstrate the powerful influence that teachers can provide when they invest effort in understanding students as individuals and as groups. They can then better support developmental changes, establish positive relationships, provide the space for identity development, and implement responsive teaching practices. When they show students that they respect them, students recognize that they care for them and respond in kind.

In the next chapter, we extend our analysis of essential developmental issues to focus more specifically on social and academic competence, two dynamics closely intertwined with personal development.

Activities for Understanding Students Better

Each chapter in *Teaching Well with Adolescent Learners* closes with example activities designed to assist you in applying the topics and concepts discussed within the chapter. The two activities that follow here (easily modified for your own needs) will help your students learn more about themselves and their class colleagues. In turn, they will assist you in better understanding your students' self-perceptions, enabling you to establish a classroom infused with an atmosphere of authentic caring.

Me Bags

One of our favorite activities for the first weeks of school is to share a Me Bag, which can work well with students of all ages. First, we teachers create our own as examples, and then we assign students to make Me Bags and bring them to share. The directions are simple:

1. Get a small paper lunch bag that you can decorate. (We often provide these for students.)

2. Decorate the outside of your bag with photos, drawings, and words that represent some of the things that are most important to you, things that people could see and know are part of your life.
3. Select one or two small objects to put inside the bag that represent important values to you, things that people might not see or know about you.
4. Plan to talk about your bag for two or three minutes.

We have found that most students are comfortable sharing their Me Bags, as most of us find it much easier to talk if we have things to show. Sometimes we ask volunteers to share with the whole class. Sometimes we share in smaller groups, depending on students' comfort levels and class size. Regardless of the format, every time we have used this activity, we have learned important things about our students' interests, friends, activities, and values. Students also learn new things about their classmates (and teachers) in a non-threatening fashion.

Another advantage of the Me Bag activity is that it can then easily transition into a content area assignment. Students can make Me Bags to represent characters in literature or history or current events, for example.

Personal Values Card Sort

There are many versions of this basic activity, most of them developed for use with individuals in a counseling setting. We have found the values card sort to be a powerful individual or small group activity that encourages reflection and discussion. Miller, C'de Baca, Matthews, and Wilbourne (2001) have shared their Personal Values Card Sort as a public domain document, and we have included it as an appendix. Teachers can structure this activity in many ways. Here is one way we have used the cards:

1. Print multiple sets of the cards so that each student in the activity has a set. (Suggestion: Laminate these to facilitate re-use or cover them with clear contact paper.)
2. In the first round, ask each student to count out the first ten cards and sort them into three piles:
   - Not important to me
   - Important to me
   - Very important to me
3. At this point, you might want to model this process with your own think-aloud commentary on some of the values, and share your own examples.
4. Also, at this point, you may want to encourage reflection, or you may choose to proceed to another round or so.
5. Reflection may be casual, such as "tell me why adventure is so important to you," or more formal, such as "write a brief paragraph that describes your most important values and gives examples."
6. Rounds may continue at different intervals, with varied directions.

This activity begins individually and may progress to small group discussions or writing activities as you wish and find beneficial to your purpose. The important aspect is that students are encouraged to think about themselves, establish priorities, and communicate with the teacher or other students. You may wish to edit the cards to fit the perspectives, and attention spans, of students. As with all activities designed to encourage sharing, your modeling as a teacher enhances effectiveness.

Appendix
Personal Values Card Sort

PERSONAL VALUES **Card Sort** W.R. Miller, J. C'de Baca, D.B. Matthews, P.L. Wilbourne University of New Mexico, 2001	**IMPORTANT TO ME**
VERY IMPORTANT TO ME	**NOT IMPORTANT TO ME**
ACCEPTANCE to be accepted as I am 1	**ACCURACY** to be accurate in my opinions and beliefs 2
ACHIEVEMENT to have important accomplishments 3	**ADVENTURE** to have new and exciting experiences 4
ATTRACTIVENESS to be physically attractive 5	**AUTHORITY** to be in charge of and responsible for others 6

AUTONOMY to be self-determined and independent 7	**BEAUTY** to appreciate beauty around me 8
CARING to take care of others 9	**CHALLENGE** to take on difficult tasks and problems 10
CHANGE to have a life full of change and variety 11	**COMFORT** to have a pleasant and comfortable life 12
COMMITMENT to make enduring, meaningful commitments 13	**COMPASSION** to feel and act on concern for others 14
CONTRIBUTION to make a lasting contribution in the world 15	**COOPERATION** to work collaboratively with others 16

17	**COURTESY** to be considerate and polite toward others	18	**CREATIVITY** to have new and original ideas
19	**DEPENDABILITY** to be reliable and trustworthy	20	**DUTY** to carry out my duties and obligations
21	**ECOLOGY** to live in harmony with the environment	22	**EXCITEMENT** to have a life full of thrills and stimulation
23	**FAITHFULNESS** to be loyal and true in relationships	24	**FAME** to be known and recognized
25	**FAMILY** to have a happy, loving family	26	**FITNESS** to be physically fit and strong

FLEXIBILITY to adjust to new circumstances easily 27	**FORGIVENESS** to be forgiving of others 28
FRIENDSHIP to have close, supportive friends 29	**FUN** to play and have fun 30
GENEROSITY to give what I have to others 31	**GENUINENESS** to act in a manner that is true to who I am 32
GOD'S WILL to seek and obey the will of God 33	**GROWTH** to keep changing and growing 34
HEALTH to be physically well and healthy 35	**HELPFULNESS** to be helpful to others 36

	HONESTY to be honest and truthful		**HOPE** to maintain a positive and optimistic outlook
37		38	
	HUMILITY to be modest and unassuming		**HUMOR** to see the humorous side of myself and the world
39		40	
	INDEPENDENCE to be free from dependence on others		**INDUSTRY** to work hard and well at my life tasks
41		42	
	INNER PEACE to experience personal peace		**INTIMACY** to share my innermost experiences with others
43		44	
	JUSTICE to promote fair and equal treatment for all		**KNOWLEDGE** to learn and contribute valuable knowledge
45		46	

LEISURE to take time to relax and enjoy 47	**LOVED** to be loved by those close to me 48
LOVING to give love to others 49	**MASTERY** to be competent in my everyday activities 50
MINDFULNESS to live conscious and mindful of the present moment 51	**MODERATION** to avoid excesses and find a middle ground 52
MONOGAMY to have one close, loving relationship 53	**NON-CONFORMITY** to question and challenge authority and norms 54
NURTURANCE to take care of and nurture others 55	**OPENNESS** to be open to new experiences, ideas, and options 56

ORDER to have a life that is well-ordered and organized 57	**PASSION** to have deep feelings about ideas, activities, or people 58
PLEASURE to feel good 59	**POPULARITY** to be well-liked by many people 60
POWER to have control over others 61	**PURPOSE** to have meaning and direction in my life 62
RATIONALITY to be guided by reason and logic 63	**REALISM** to see and act realistically and practically 64
RESPONSIBILITY to make and carry out responsible decisions 65	**RISK** to take risks and chances 66

67	**ROMANCE** to have intense, exciting love in my life	69	**SAFETY** to be safe and secure
68	**SELF-ACCEPTANCE** to accept myself as I am	70	**SELF-CONTROL** to be disciplined in my own actions
71	**SELF-ESTEEM** to feel good about myself	72	**SELF-KNOWLEDGE** to have a deep and honest understanding of myself
73	**SERVICE** to be of service to others	74	**SEXUALITY** to have an active and satisfying sex life
75	**SIMPLICITY** to live life simply, with minimal needs	76	**SOLITUDE** to have time and space where I can be apart from others

SPIRITUALITY to grow and mature spiritually 77	**STABILITY** to have a life that stays fairly consistent 78
TOLERANCE to accept and respect those who differ from me 79	**TRADITION** to follow respected patterns of the past 80
VIRTUE to live a morally pure and excellent life 81	**WEALTH** to have plenty of money 82
WORLD PEACE to work to promote peace in the world 83	**Other Value:**
Other Value:	**Other Value:**

This instrument is in the public domain and may be copied adapted and used without permission.

References

Anderson, M., & Jiang, J. (2018). *Teens, Social Media & Technology 2018*. Washington, DC: Pew Internet & American Life Project.

Benson, P.L., Leffert, N., Scales, P.C., & Blyth, D.A. (1998). Beyond the "Village" Rhetoric: Creating Healthy Communities for Children and Adolescents, *Applied Developmental Science*, 2, 138–159.

Crone, E. (2017). *The Adolescent Brain: Changes in Learning, Decision-Making, and Social Relations*. New York, NY: Routledge.

DePaul University. (n.d.). *Activities for Metacognition*. Activities for Metacognition | Learning Activities | Teaching Guides | Teaching Commons | DePaul University, Chicago. Retrieved January 19, 2022, from https://resources.depaul.edu/teaching-commons/teaching-guides/learning-activities/Pages/activities-for-metacognition.aspx

Dunn, D. & Burcaw, S. (2013). Disability identity: Exploring Narrative Accounts of Disability. *Rehabilitation Psychology*, 58(2), 148–157.

Erikson, E. (1959). *Identity and the Life Cycle*. New York, NY: International Universities Press.

Gardner, H., and Davis, K. (2013). *The App Generation: How Today's Youth Navigate Identity, Intimacy, and Imagination In A Digital World*. New Haven, CT: Yale University Press.

Horn, I.S. (2008). Turnaround Students in High School Mathematics: Constructing Identities of Competence Through Mathematical Worlds. *Mathematical Thinking and Learning*, 10(3), 201–239.

Huang, C.Y., & Stormshak, E.A. (2011). A Longitudinal Examination of Early Adolescence Ethnic Identity Trajectories. *Cultural Diversity & Ethnic Minority Psychology*, 17, 261–270.

Lee, H. (1960). *To Kill a Mockingbird*. Philadelphia, PA: Lippincott.

Masten, A.S., Best, K.M., & Garmezy, N. (1990) Resilience and Development: Contributions from the Study of Children Who Overcome Adversity. *Development and Psychopathology*, 2, 425–444.

Miller, W.R., C'de Baca, J., Matthews, P. & Wilbourne, P. (2001). Personal Values Card Sort. University of New Mexico. https://motivational-interviewing.org/content/personal-values-card-sort

Mueller, C.O., (2021) "I Didn't Know People With Disabilities Could Grow Up To Be Adults": Disability History, Curriculum, and Identity in Special Education. *Teacher Education and Special Education*, 1–17.

National Academies of Sciences, Engineering, and Medicine. (2019). *The Promise Of Adolescence: Realizing Opportunity for All Youth.* Washington, DC: The National Academies Press. https://doi.org/10.17226/25388

Rivas-Drake, D., Syed, M., Umaña-Taylor, A.J., Markstrom, C., French, S., Schwartz, S.J., & Ethnic and Racial Identity in the 21st Century Study Group. (2014). Feeling Good, Happy, and Proud: A Meta-Analysis of Positive Ethnic-Racial Affect and Adjustment Among Diverse Children and Adolescents. *Child Development*, 85, 77–102.

Rivas-Drake, D., & Umaña-Taylor, A.J. (2019). How Do Youth Form Their Ideas About Ethnicity and Race? In D. Rivas-Drake & A. J. Umaña-Taylor, Eds., *Below the Surface: Talking With Teens About Race, Ethnicity, and Identity.* Princeton, NJ: Princeton University Press, 71–98.

Stevens, A.P. (2017, October) The Power Of "Like." *Science News for Students.* Society for Science & the Public.

Turner, K.H., Hicks, T., & Zucker, L. (2019). Connected Reading: A Framework for Understanding How Adolescents Encounter, Evaluate, And Engage With Texts in the Digital Age. *Reading Research Quarterly*, 55(2), 291–309. doi:10.1002/rrq.271

Umaña-Taylor, A.J., Quintana, S.M., Lee, R.M., Cross, W.E., Rivas-Drake, D., Schwartz, S.J., Syed, M., Yip, T., & Seaton, E. (2014). Ethnic and Racial Identity During Adolescence and into Young Adulthood: An Integrated Conceptualization. *Child Development*, 85(1), 21–39.

Verhoeven, M., Poorthuis, A.M.G., & Volman, M. (2018). The Role of School in Adolescents' Identity Development. A Literature Review. *Educational Psychology Review*, 2019, 31, 35–63. https://doi.org/10.1007/s10648-018-9457-3

Wang, J., Zhang, D., & Zimmerman, M.A. (2015). Resilience Theory and its Implications for Chinese Adolescents. *Psychological Reports: Disability & Trauma*, 117(2), 354–375.

5

Relating and Persevering
Patterns of Social and Moral Development

In our previous chapters, we have described some of the most important dynamics in adolescent development. We have shown how changes in brains and bodies enable new accomplishments and new ways of thinking. We have stressed the variability of these experiences and adolescents' perceptions of them. Repeatedly, we have emphasized the power of context, how changes are determined by both internal and external factors, nature and nurture.

This interplay is especially important with social and moral development. How adolescents relate to others and how others relate to them impacts their identity and their development of competence, both social and academic. Adults who provide the types of authentic caring we have advocated can make profound differences in the lives of adolescents as they negotiate these changes (Rivas-Drake & Umaña-Taylor, 2019). Conversely, when adolescents experience harm or negligence, healthy development can be comprised.

In this chapter, we examine the risks and benefits of relationships, especially as they relate to the development of social and academic competence.

Gaining Social and Academic Competence

As we demonstrated in the preceding chapter, identity development is an interactive and negotiated process. These same processes characterize the development of social and academic competence. Students try to make sense of information about who they are as friends, how they relate to people, how well they perform academically, and who they are in school. In the next section of this chapter, we examine more specifically how the sense of self as a friend and sense of self as a student develop in a connected fashion.

Social Competence

Peer dynamics greatly influence the negotiation of all aspects of identity. Everyone who spends time with adolescents recognizes the importance of peer relationships. As students progress through the grades, teachers notice dramatic shifts in their social interactions. The spontaneous play we see on the playgrounds in elementary school and spur-of-the-moment conversations we hear in those lunchrooms give way to more intense social interactions in middle and high school. Who sits with whom, who is friends with whom, and how groups form become serious issues that shape perceptions of identity.

As a general pattern, concerns about social status and popularity become more pronounced. In some cases, excessive attention to social status can lead to hierarchical, segregated learning spaces (Wilson, Karimpour, & Rodkin, 2011). In the social world of adolescents, young people who are "influencers" become especially significant. These are the students who determine what is cool or uncool, trendy or blasé, sometimes through explicit statements, sometimes simply by what they do and wear. In some situations, their leadership status provides positive role modeling. In others, they may draw students off task. Paluck, Shepherd, and Aronow (2016) suggest that teachers realize that influencers are often natural leaders and try to find ways for them to strengthen their leadership skills, perhaps enlisting them in efforts to enhance school climate, such as reducing bullying. Teachers have also found these influential adolescents can promote positive attitudes toward academics and provide classroom leadership in general.

Learning more about peer influences can help us better understand the social dynamics in our classrooms. In a three-year longitudinal study with 316 African American young adolescents living in high-risk neighborhoods, Quimby, Richards, Santiago, Scott, and Puvar (2017) explored relationships among peer association, ethnic identity, and gender. For the purposes of their study, they defined peer influence as "a way of intentionally or unintentionally transmitting a group's attitudes so that a person is encouraged to be consistent with the group's norms" (p. 712).

> In order to fit in and be accepted, adolescents often succumb to this influence. This influence is of particular importance in early, as opposed to late, adolescence, when youth tend to be most easily swayed by their peers due to the development of reward mechanisms in the brain that precedes control mechanisms.
>
> (p. 712)

The researchers investigated the dynamics of peer association. In contrast to direct influences from specific individuals, peer association is more broadly contextual, related to the behaviors of the peers in the immediate community. To capture perceptions of peer associations as they experienced different influences—in school, after school, community connections, informal gatherings—researchers used an "experience sampling methodology." Participants received watches programmed to alert them to respond to questions in a notebook at random intervals. When prompted, participants recorded where they were, what they were doing, and whom they were with.

Working from the positive youth development theory framed by Developmental Assets (Benson, Leffert, Scales, & Blyth, 1998), researchers examined relationships between positive peer association and measures of self-esteem, school connectedness, parental relationship, and normative beliefs about aggression. They found that as positive peer association increased from sixth to eighth grade, participants reported higher levels of self-esteem, school connectedness, paternal and maternal closeness, and a decrease in supportive beliefs about aggression.

Participants who experienced more stable positive peer associations reported even higher levels of self-esteem and school connectedness. Participants with stronger ethnic-racial identities showed more positive outcomes across time. Results were consistent for boys and girls with no significant differences by gender. Researchers concluded that peer influence can strengthen health and wellness among adolescents and may be especially important for young people in less advantaged settings.

Crone (2017) reviewed sociological analyses of adolescent behavior to provide clearer descriptions of social development. "Prosocial behavior" is essential.

> Prosocial behavior is described as voluntary behavior to benefit others, and has a major role in strengthening social ties between individuals, which is crucial for the formation and continuation of friendships. Given that adolescence is the period in life when individuals develop more intimate friendships, important changes in prosocial development is expected as well.
>
> (p. 137)

Figure 5.1 Celebrating teamwork

Her research describes the formation of friendships as a complex process. Successful friendships require abilities to recognize emotions in others, establish a place within a group, deal with feelings of acceptance and rejection, and consider the perspectives of others. Studies show a wide range of individual differences in these developments. Context and environment are critical factors. Some adolescents are especially susceptible to frustrating experiences, especially in non-supportive environments. Children who have grown up surrounded by people who demonstrate strong prosocial behaviors—people who listen to each other, laugh together, and support each other when they experience negative life experiences—are far more likely to develop these behaviors as they get to know new people in school. Children who grew up with less frequent social experiences may find meeting new people more intimidating.

Academic Competence

Perceptions of academic competence are shaped by social comparison in the same ways as other aspects of identity. In the early grades, students observe how well others do in lessons and form self-perceptions accordingly. They soon learn who reads well and who does not, who gets to work independently and who needs help, who goes to enrichment and who goes to remediation. If an observer were to ask a student in a third-grade classroom to rank order the reading levels of his 25 classmates from highest to lowest, he could probably do so accurately.

Social comparisons become more intense in upper elementary grades and are generally set by high school. Some students begin to adopt coping behaviors to try to offset negative comparisons. For example, a student can try to save face by repeatedly forgetting to submit an assignment rather than admitting she did not understand it. That same student might want to use the bathroom pass frequently rather than sit through a discussion that she finds confusing.

At the same time that social comparisons drive avoidance, they can also fuel competition. Observant teachers pick up on these clues and try to respond thoughtfully. They realize that comments they make and comments from classmates become especially powerful. Successful teachers understand the development of identity as a negotiated process, especially as it relates to perceptions of self as a student. In a positive classroom environment, students encourage and support each other without engaging in competition for social status.

A useful analogy for thinking about the dynamics of the negotiation of academic competence is the "poker chip theory" of self-concept suggested by Canfield and Wells (1976). The notion is that students approach academic tasks with a self-concept similar to the ways a poker player approaches a hand. Successful experiences from previous lessons create a big stack of chips and empower students to take risks. For example, a student who has done well in math games is likely to jump right in when it is game time again. He can afford to risk an answer being wrong. A student who has not done well in these games has much fewer chips. He is not likely to gamble unless he sees a question as a sure thing. This analogy helps explain why some students readily engage with lesson tasks, and some do not. It also reminds us that self-concept may vary from day to day and from task to task.

Over the past decade, a growing body of research has examined the mindsets students bring to academic tasks. In general terms, a mindset is "a complex mental state involving beliefs and feelings and values and dispositions to act in certain ways" (https://www.vocabulary.com/dictionary/mindset). Teachers recognize the power of mindsets in shaping behavior. If a student believes she is "not a math person," she begins a new school year from a deficit perspective. If, on the other hand, she approaches new math problems with confidence, she will look forward to a more challenging course.

Mindsets affect motivation, receptiveness to learning, and level of achievement. Longitudinal studies have shown that the extent to which students believe that intelligence is fixed or malleable predicts achievement or underachievement rates (Dweck, 2008; Lee, Heeter, Magerko, & Medler, 2012; Boaler, 2013). Students with fixed mindsets often view success as a verification of their intelligence. Good grades and high test scores show them how smart they are. When tasks become more challenging, students with fixed mindsets may prefer activities that would make them look smart over those that would bring new challenges (Dweck, 2010). When pressed, they may question their abilities and resort to negative strategies, like cheating or lying about their successes. In contrast, students with growth mindsets recognize that they can improve their abilities by working harder.

Over time, mindsets contribute to broader learning dispositions (Farrington et al., 2012). Students with a history of success have developed a set of academic behaviors. They engage with learning activities, pay attention, participate in class, and complete homework. These behaviors become habits for them, enabling the academic perseverance needed to accomplish challenging tasks.

To understand better just how these dynamics occur in lessons, Strahan, Hansen, Doherty, Meyer, and Buchanan (2017) conducted case studies with 12 seventh graders in a language arts class across a school year. In her lessons, the teacher integrated the exploration of four aspects of mindsets with reading and writing: belief that learning abilities can grow with the investment of effort, willingness to address challenging tasks and persevere, development of stronger learning strategies, and ability to articulate connections between effort and accomplishment.

Participants in these case studies expressed connections among concepts in different ways. Six of them understood all four aspects of the mindsets emphasized. These students expressed connections among their thoughts and actions, using their experiences with dance, music, and sports to describe specific instances when they thought about effort and accomplishment. Susan, for example, shared her passion for music and drama. She connected her interest in music with her work in school.

> I can hear a song once or twice and it stays in my brain. I know that's kind of crazy, but I can hear a song on the radio and it can be old or new, and I haven't heard it often, but I can still sing along to it. So sometimes if I have to study for something, I would turn it into songs just so I can remember.
>
> (p. 7)

In one of her essays, she wrote:

> If you have a fixed mindset and think negatively about school, then that could affect your work. A growth mindset is when you believe you can do things and believe that you can grow academically. In my opinion, a growth mindset seems completely necessary because if you believe that you can't grow and don't show effort, then you can't and won't, in most cases, do your very best. This leads me to believe that the more effort you invest, the more potential you have to become even smarter.
>
> (p. 7)

The other six seventh graders made connections that varied by subject matter. Sarah, for example, sometimes described herself as a diligent learner yet she described her perceived weaknesses more often than her strengths. When asked to describe the most important aspects of mental preparation for exams, she responded, "Knowing that no matter what, I could study for weeks and weeks and weeks but what I know is what I know and what I get is what I get." She went on to say,

> Well, it depends on which test. With the science test, I reread and I went through it and took the test again just to make sure I did everything right cause it was a simple test and didn't take very long. But the reading and math, I didn't have time to do that—they took too long. When I was doing them, I would mark them [challenging questions] with a star and then go back to them.
>
> (p. 12)

She provided additional explanation in one of her essays,

> I grew up being told that I can never learn too much. When I was in elementary school, until second grade, I was behind two grade levels. Then I had a teacher and a

tutor that helped me get on track. They found that I memorized things very well ... You can keep learning things until you refuse to. Every student can become engaged with a topic and learn more things about that topic. Each of us can grow stronger if we try, in school or out. The more effort I invest, the more I learn, the more I grow.

(p. 12)

Investigations of the nature and power of mindsets have helped us better understand the relationships among attitudes and behaviors that constitute academic competence. Developing strong academic mindsets enhances a more resilient sense of self, extending the development of personal power, self-esteem, sense of purpose and positive views of personal future.

Negative mindsets, in contrast, may lead to a sense of learned helplessness. As the name suggests, students who have developed a habit of learned helplessness often respond to academic tasks by disengaging from lessons. They have internalized a belief that they are incapable of succeeding and often choose avoidance as a means of risking failure (Filipello, Buzzai, Costa, Orecchio, & Sorrenti, 2020).

In an effective classroom, teachers try to find ways to create connections with students who have developed such negative mindsets. Amie Broyhill's narrative report of her interactions with one of her students shows how she negotiated these complex dynamics in real time.

Classroom Narrative: Encouraging Competency—Anthony's Case

By Amie Broyhill, The Catamount School, Sylva, NC

As we planned our Project Based Learning units, we emphasized student agency, mastery, and deeper learning of content and skills, while promoting real-world problem-solving skills. We realized that PBL can be complex and often requires low-stakes learning to master time management, organization, and collaboration skills required to solve problems. As we taught our unit on environment and ecology, I had an opportunity to experience the power of incorporating real-world learning into our academic content.

These insights began with one of our students who was developing severe learned helplessness and falling behind in all his classes. Anthony came to us with a thick virtual file of assessments from fifth grade. He struggled with reading and mathematics and had not done well on any of his achievement tests. One-on-one interventions had not proven especially productive. As we soon learned, Anthony was difficult to engage in lessons. He gave off an aura that everything was boring and unnecessary. He began to accumulate a stack of behavioral referrals, mostly for disrupting group work and calling out to his friends. During the first semester, when we were studying the Mesoamerican cultures, his demeanor changed drastically when we brought out the tools and paints for projects. He was energized and present. He engaged with his team and contributed to a good project constructing temples with various materials such as sugar cubes and cardboard. He engaged in papier-mâché to replicate mosaic masks of the Mayas. Anthony went on to construct different weapons and tools used by the Mesoamerican tribes, learning to build trust with the classroom teacher to use hand tools, spray paint, and work outside in small groups.

As we discussed Anthony's situation in our team meetings, we agreed that his stress in lessons led to shutdown and then to defiance. We designed a targeted intervention that focused on goal setting, and I agreed to work with him during flextime. Our first meeting was unproductive because my ideas failed to rouse any motivation or focus. For the next two meetings, I came in with a more structured plan of targeted tasks, which felt like pulling teeth.

By the end of the third meeting, the defiance began to turn to minor disrespect. My frustration allowed this to weigh on me, and, through conversations with personal family, peers, and fellow teachers, I concluded that I needed to build something to address his reoccurring defense: "Why do I have to do this?" "Why do I have to learn this stuff?" My responses emphasizing the importance of turning your work in on time and getting good grades fell on deaf ears. Fearing repercussions from school and home seemed to be fleeting concerns. I learned that Anthony spent a lot of time with his grandfather building and constructing different things, repairing and working with various materials in their time together. He valued this time dearly. It was one of the few topics he shared with enthusiasm. Given that our school-wide PBL focused on campus ecology and community gardens, I decided to try an experiment with Anthony.

Our fourth meeting came to an abrupt start with me dropping wood, screws, tools, and bench schematics at his feet in our outdoor space. He was confused and I gave very few instructions. I said, "Build it." At first, he shrugged off my request and opened the schematics. I chose a simple design and amended the plans with additional literacy tools such as an index, dictionary, and table of contents. I also provided two or three *how-to* guides on different steps within the bench schematics, such as how to use a compound miter saw and instructions on how to use a speed square. I purposely designed the notebook to keep the references in the back and to have the book open directly to the schematics after the table of contents.

Anthony stared at the paper for a while. He picked up some materials and fiddled with them. I stood by patiently and watched him. He went from being incredibly confident in his surroundings to feeling unprepared as he started to read the building plans. It took the better part of 20 minutes for him to tell me he didn't know what to do. I inquired why that was when I knew he spent a lot of his time building different things with his grandfather. He explained that his grandfather just told him what to do and showed him how to do it. I asked him what his goals were after he finished school, and he said to do something in the field of lumbering or woodworking. I asked him how he was going to do this if he didn't learn to read at that level or understand how to complete the mathematics required by the schematics. I think he felt somewhat embarrassed, but our relationship became more authentic from that conversation.

I followed with a quick anecdote about how I used to work with my dad in the garage growing up, but I realized I couldn't do it without him right next to me unless he stopped showing me, and I started to do these things for myself. I told him I specifically struggled with the mathematics of it all. I asked him if he wanted to build the bench together and he agreed. Over the next few weeks, we constructed two Adirondack benches.

Six months later, the benches sit outside my classroom. What matters most is that I never heard, "Why do I have to learn this?" again. Instead, Anthony continued to struggle, but he put forth genuine effort in most of his academic and personal choices. He was rarely argumentative or defiant.

I learned that the authenticity of the problem can make a difference for students and take learning from a figurative realm to a literal reality. When it is a problem that directly shakes their foundation or charges their inner drive, their motivation can change. Although I had not designed our intervention as a PBL per se, it became the most authentic and most successful PBL of my career. The metacognition naturally occurred while we fought the saw. Goal setting conversations came at the end of our work sessions as we shook sawdust off our clothes and shoes. We encouraged other students to come to help us at times, and Anthony began to bridge his relationship with his peers. Our administrator got to see Anthony in a new light after months of discussions about his decisions. It was never a fix-all, but it was an important step we took together.

As was the case with the previous narrative "Supporting Charlotte and Her Classmates," like Charlotte's teacher, Anthony's teacher embodies a stance of authentic caring. The relationship she established with Anthony enabled her to identify his strengths and interests in building things. She found a meaningful way to integrate bench building with the PBL efforts to enhance the school grounds. Because he had learned to trust her, Anthony was willing to take chances with reading schematics and how-to guides. Working side-by-side strengthened trust. As a result, the benches they built together became concrete, tangible proof of accomplishment.

A Small Steps Approach to Social and Academic Competence
With both social and academic competence, students experience success in a similar fashion. To gain confidence, students need a delicate combination of encouragement and coaching, a process

similar to learning to walk, which teachers might consider a "small steps approach."

From any natural learning situation, whether it is learning to walk, to ride a bicycle, or to drive a car, we can draw essential insights. Several key dynamics occur. To take their first steps, babies need some sense of what walking is, that is, a sense of purpose. The learner also needs to feel safe to be able to use feedback from the task itself to improve performance. Babies and bicycle riders lose their balance and fall down. Drivers learn to avoid under steering or over braking in a parking lot. To get back from a fall, some encouragement and reassurance is helpful. From a teaching perspective, we might agree that the focus is on the learning rather than the teaching.

Anthony's narrative, like those in other chapters, provides a clear illustration of the dynamics of engagement. Students who engaged most with new social situations and academic tasks were those who 1) learned to reflect more thoughtfully about their own thinking and their own engagement and 2) began to feel a sense of ownership for their own learning. Their comments in interviews showed that these two essential dynamics, reflection and ownership, are closely intertwined. Thinking about their engagement decisions enabled them to realize that they had a personal stake in the process, and, as they internalized a sense of progress, their ownership of their learning grew stronger. Using the "poker chip" analogy, small successes with peers and academic tasks add chips to the stack of self-esteem.

From a research perspective, reflection has much to do with "self-awareness" and ownership with "agency." Self-awareness is one of the core SEL competencies identified by the Collaborative for Academic, Social, and Emotional Learning (CASEL; Pennsylvania State University, 2017).

> Self-awareness is the ability to accurately recognize one's own emotions, thoughts, and values and how they influence behavior. The ability to accurately assess one's strengths and limitations, with a well-grounded sense of confidence, optimism, and a "growth mindset."
>
> (The Pennsylvania State University, October 2017, p. 4)

Agency is one of the central social/emotional factors for school success.

> Agency is the ability to make choices about and take an active role in one's life path, rather than solely being the product of one's circumstances. Agency requires the intentionality and forethought to derive a course of action and adjust course as needed to reflect one's identity, competencies, knowledge and skills, mindsets, and values.
> (Nagaoka, Farrington, Ehrlich, & Heath, 2015, p. 2)

From the perspectives of both research and wisdom of practice, a small steps approach to connecting with students might enable teachers to provide more natural and meaningful support. As illustrated in Amy Broyhill's work with Anthony, small steps might include

1. Establishing trusting relationships with students
2. Engaging students in conversations about themselves and their work in school
3. Designing lesson activities that scaffold instruction in small steps that can be accomplished successfully
4. Offering encouragement and support as students engage with activities
5. Encouraging students to set personal and academic goals, then reflecting on progress toward these goals
6. Providing choices of assignments and projects

Expanding Perspectives and Promoting Ethics

In this chapter, we have described how powerful patterns of personal and social development shape students' growth toward becoming caring, responsible adults. As cognitive abilities grow more sophisticated, adolescents develop capacities for understanding better who they are, how they relate to others, and how they achieve competence. Successful experiences enhance self-awareness and agency. Together, these developments enable new levels of perspective and possibilities for moral development.

Ways children learn concepts of right and wrong and develop notions of justice have intrigued psychologists for more than a century. Early theories that focused on sequential stages have given way to more interactive and contextual approaches. We now understand that empathy is the heart of moral behavior. Children begin to exhibit empathy at an early age. For example, the cries of a child in one area of a nursery may trigger responses from other infants. Toddlers offer gifts to others and share belongings. With preschoolers, teachers see the give-and-take of learning empathy every day on the playground. When it comes to popular toys, sometimes it is literally a give and take. While parents and caregivers encourage sharing explicitly, we also understand the power of social learning. Children watch each other and mimic others they wish to emulate. Modeling may be the most powerful influence on emotional self-regulation.

Alongside the development of empathy, we observe early notions of rights and wrongs, do's and don'ts, rules and expectations. For a time, children express concrete concepts of justice and tend to perceive social situations in black-and-white terms. As thinking grows more powerful, children begin to observe nuance and sense that rules can be negotiated. The concept of intentionality becomes more important, and, by the time they begin school, most children have a sense that mistakes done "on purpose" are worse than accidents.

As children approach adolescence, growing powers of reasoning make possible interpretations that are more complex.

> In order to fathom other people's thoughts and intentions, it is essential that you are able to understand intentions and motives, to consider different options, and to think about the consequences of your actions for yourself and your social environment, like your circle of friends or your family. So, in addition to offering all sorts of possibilities for academic learning, the increase in cognitive abilities is also important at this stage in life for being able to take the perspective of others.
>
> (Crone, 2017, p. 113)

As with other aspects of thinking, changes in the brain enable more sophisticated social perspective-taking. In studies of brains in action during social dilemmas, adolescents made more systematic and strategic choices than children did. Being able to take the perspective of another person becomes more automatic. "So, during adolescence, we see a gradual transition from dominance by the self-area (medial prefrontal cortex: thinking about yourself) to dominance by the other-area (the temporoparietal junction; taking the perspective of the other)" (Crone, 2017, p. 123).

Based on these general dynamics, mature perspective-taking becomes possible in later adolescence. Essential skills include projecting situations into the future, seeing different angles, and putting things into perspective. These skills enable a sense of autonomy—knowing that one can make independent decisions and take care of oneself.

As Dru Tomlin (2017) suggested in his blog post for Middle Level Education Month,

> Adolescents are beginning to see their immediate world and the larger world as the morally complicated landscapes they are. As a result, our students are often at conflict with the world as it is and the world as they think/hope/dream it should be. Their "moral thermometers" are

Figure 5.2 Mature perspective-taking

still taking shape as they gauge the ethical temperature of a situation; therefore, in their search for justice, they sometimes are quick to measure others' flaws while they are slow to see those same flaws in themselves. That's why we have students who are able to grasp society's missteps (and its magnificence) and help peers solve conflicts as well as students who are raging because they feel like no one gets them, the world is totally messed up, and they are all alone. (http://www.amle.org/BrowsebyTopic/WhatsNew/WNDet.aspx?ArtMID=888&ArticleID=788)

While these general patterns describe changes for groups, individuals vary greatly in the extent to which they make sense of social situations and demonstrate moral reasoning. As with all aspects of personal and social development, life experiences are essential. Participants in studies of the development of empathy express major differences depending on their experiences in observing empathy with family members or friends.

Recent studies on the development of empathy suggest that, like other aspects of personal and social development, adolescents negotiate values and perspectives as they interact with significant others and life experiences. A key aspect of this development is prosocial behavior, which generally is defined as voluntary behavior intended to benefit others (Van der Graaf, Carlo, Crocetti, Koot, & Branje, 2017). Such behavior is clearly a developmental asset, strongly associated with high self-esteem, academic success, and positive social relationships.

From a theoretical perspective, empathy provides the motivational energy necessary to engage in prosocial behavior. Helping behaviors stem from understanding others' perspectives and feeling concern for them. As with many behaviors and attitudes, the act of helping someone probably enhances perspective-taking and empathy, fueling a growth spiral of sorts. Helping behaviors are reinforced by positive feedback from adults and peers, which reinforces perceptions of self as caring persons, which further encourages helping behaviors. In optimal situations, these dynamics result in a more integrated sense of self and a strong moral identity (Carlo, Padilla-Walker, & Nielson, 2015).

Adolescence is a critical time for this growth as physical maturity and increased autonomy makes it possible to engage in more prosocial behaviors. Growing powers of reasoning enable reflection, which strengthens values. Given the differences in the ways boys and girls experience social expectations, it is likely that the development of prosocial behaviors differs by gender, with girls socialized to show more nurturance and caring.

In a longitudinal study with 497 young people in the Netherlands, Van der Graaf, Carlo, Crocetti, Koot, and Branje (2017) explored relationships between prosocial behavior and empathy across the time from middle adolescence (junior high or middle school) through graduation from high school. Prosocial behaviors were assessed with survey items such as "I'm willing to lend money to others if they really need it," and "I try to get others involved in group activities" (p. 1089); perspective-taking with items such as "I try to look at everybody's side of a disagreement before I make a decision," and empathic concern with items such as "I often have tender, concerned feelings for people less fortunate than me" (p. 1090). Results indicated that prosocial behaviors increased until mid-adolescence and then decreased slightly as participants transitioned into early adulthood. Girls reported more prosocial behaviors at earlier ages and showed stronger associations among empathic concern, perspective-taking, and prosocial behavior. Researchers concluded that educators might best encourage prosocial behaviors by focusing on promoting empathic concern and perspective-taking.

Providing the time and guidance needed for students to explore and develop these traits is an important part of adolescence, though it can be difficult. The results are worthy, however, as they help ensure a deeper sense of personal confidence, longer-lasting relationships, and the perseverance needed for a healthier adulthood. Let us turn again to Jeanneine's classroom, where we find an illustration of empathic concern and perspective-taking.

As has become clear from other chapters, my eighth graders were precious to me, though they definitely weren't living their best lives. They could be just as hateful to each other as you'd imagine from your own experiences, and this was actually common across all grade levels in the building. The faculty decided to band together to address some specific behavioral concerns we were witnessing in the wayside times of lunch, social breaks, ballgames, and bathrooms, and we felt like empathy, perspective, compassion, understanding, trust, and viewpoint were all words that every adolescent should know and be held accountable for in appropriate measure. We had an advisory period in my school, perhaps an early form of the Social Emotional Learning curriculum prevalent today, and we used that 20 minutes in the early morning to address lots of things, like yesterday's fight in the cafeteria, protocols to follow when our school had guests from the district office, and especially the moral obligations of borrowing school supplies from my desk that it seemed like nobody ever returned. All much easier said than done.

I found that teaching empathy was tough stuff. Unless an adolescent is there—there in that place where he or she can think abstractly, make emotional connections, consider consequences, has a handle on perspective-taking, can really do the "walk a mile in my shoes" kind of thinking—well, it's hard to quantify the streams of thought that lead an adolescent to understand the concept of empathy. I just wasn't sure they were at that level of maturity. But like a good soldier, I plunged in. As an ELA teacher, I already had the advantage of designing many novel studies and teaching selected short stories and other genres, so talking about viewpoint was in my wheelhouse, a common discussion when we laid certain literary elements over a reading.

We now began to bear down on the perspectives of those fictional characters and the way they interacted with each other in terms of feelings and responses. I used the word empathy frequently and deliberately in class. We defined it. We researched the psychology behind it. We talked about better understanding our own feelings to empathize with others. We built a word wall, discussed perspective-taking as a forerunner to empathy, talked about its innateness, posted sticky notes that captured examples of empathy they witnessed, and filled journal pages. We talked openly about stereotypes and biases surrounding race and ethnicity, and we unpacked relevant myths and misinformation about those who, first look, appear different.

We role played in advisory and used agreed-upon common steps: recognizing a need in another, then imaging how that person felt, next talking about it using open-ended questions, confirming everything through body language and active listening, and finally responding to the situation appropriately and maybe with follow up. From there we did Quick Writes or Turn and Talks that debriefed personally before whole-group closure.

Truth be told, I wasn't sure how much impact these activities were actually having, though, so we finished up and moved on to other lessons.

Fast forward about three months.

I have no idea what the situation was that led to this event, and, frankly, I don't even remember the topic I was teaching. I do recall that it was in the early spring and, as had become my habit, I had shifted the label I used on my students. I never called them kids or children (they'll be what you expect them to be), and instead I had referred to them across the fall as young adults. I now began to call them pre-high schoolers because that's where they were headed and I wanted to get them socially and emotionally ready for all the freedoms they'd face from grade nine on. Part of this shift was giving them more responsibility, so they began to lead class discussions and formally reinforce new concepts in peer and whole-group teaching.

On that particular day it was Lettie's turn to lead discussion. Smart, articulate, gregarious and gorgeous, sensitive, and unassuming ... she was every girl's wanna-be. You'd look at Lettie and think her life was one big bundle of future, but somewhere in that moment we all learned otherwise. She was doing whatever she was doing when she abruptly stopped, teared up, and just kind of announced right out loud that her mom was anorexic and how it was totally devastating her family. She tumbled into this emotional space, and I mean she really, really tumbled, words and feelings all spilling out in a gush.

I was sitting in the back row and suddenly found that I couldn't breathe. What should I say? How should I handle this? What were the kids going to do in reaction? How fast would this raw, vulnerable admission go sideways in this place of 14-year-olds? Every teacher responsible for a classroom has those flashes of panic, knowing she has to be the front line yet not being sure how to handle the emotional situation.

Turns out I never said a word. In that moment, my kids were beautiful. I can still picture their responses to her. First, one classmate asked a question, and then another said something very appropriate, then a third chimed in and asked how that made Lettie's younger brother feel, and a fourth shared a similar experience, another asked how he could help—and so it went until a few actually went up to hug her. That was their time, not mine. There was nothing for me to offer, to say or do; it was all them—30 friends in the same space and place, as different as any 30 teenagers could be, yet feeling and empathizing and all being the same person. I softly invited them to step outside the back door onto my classroom patio and take a minute. Their heart for Lettie, the way they talked with her as one adult might talk to another, as one friend would feel her hurt and validate that feeling, well—that was beyond measure. I watched them from the huge window of my classroom and in that moment knew they would all make it just fine.

In this scenario, we see a class of 30 adolescents who, though it did not seem likely at the time, absorbed targeted instruction on perspective-taking and empathy and were able to internalize and apply that as appropriate to the situation and their developmental levels of understanding. As teachers, we might be inclined to steer away from teaching topics such as these, yet their positive influence on classroom dynamics cannot be overlooked. Building healthy relationships, managing emotions, strengthening social skills, and reaching out in kindness are important markers in the journey to a strong and productive adulthood.

Conclusions

As with identity development, social and moral development happen as individuals interact with their environment. When provided physical safety and emotional security, young people can explore new ways of relating with others and engage with challenging academic tasks. The poker chip theory of self-concept suggested by Canfield and Wells (1976) is a strong metaphor for these dynamics. Safe, successful experiences build the confidence needed to take risks—meeting new people, trying new activities, taking on academic challenges. With a short supply of confidence, protecting oneself and playing it safe become paramount. Developing resiliency requires both internal strength and social support.

As adolescents think about their interactions with others, concerns about social status and popularity typically become more pronounced. Positive peer association encourages self-esteem and school connectedness. Successful friendships require abilities to recognize emotions in others, establish a place within a group, deal with feelings of acceptance and rejection, and consider the perspectives of others.

Academic competence grows in a similar interactive fashion. Students with a history of success engage with learning activities, pay attention, participate in class, and complete homework. These behaviors become habits for them, enabling the academic perseverance needed to accomplish challenging tasks. Students who engage most with new social situations and academic tasks are those who 1) learn to reflect more thoughtfully about their own thinking and their own engagement and 2) begin to feel a sense of ownership for their own learning.

Adolescents strengthen concepts of right and wrong and develop notions of justice in ways that are also interactive and contextual. During adolescence, we see a gradual transition from perspectives dominated by self toward perspectives that include others. Essential skills include projecting situations into the future, seeing different angles, and putting things into perspective. These skills enable a sense of autonomy—knowing that one can make independent decisions and take care of oneself. Growing powers of reasoning enable reflection, which strengthens values. One of the most visible changes is an increasing capacity for empathy, both in the abstract with vicarious experiences and in the day-to-day interactions with peers and family members.

These interactive dynamics of social relationships, academic competence, and moral development demonstrate the forces at work in our Framework for Teaching Well with Adolescent Learners. Safety and trust are essential preconditions. Teachers who understand and support developmental changes, create positive relationships, and implement responsive practices become powerful influences for growing more resilient. These dynamics also demonstrate the interplay of internal and external developmental assets. Support from caring adults, community resources, and a positive classroom climate enable social skills and academic achievement. In the next chapter, we will examine, in detail, the important ways schools can enhance these supportive conditions.

Activities for Understanding Students Better

The activities that follow will help your students learn more about themselves and their classmates, and they will assist you in learning more about your students' personal and social self-perceptions.

Exploring Images and Stereotypes

A good way to help students better understand identity issues is to examine cultural images and stereotypes. By thinking critically about images and sharing their emotional responses, students can consider ways that cultural messages affect their views of themselves and reflect on their values. We like to approach these activities in two phases. In the first phase, we select images that may prompt a range of responses. To integrate these activities, we select images that relate to our curricular focus, for example, in a unit on a novel like *The Outsiders*, *Speak*, *Black Like Me*, *The Hate U Give*, or *The Scarlet Letter*. We might find six images of young people with different styles of clothing and hair that might suggest stereotypes about social class, ingroups, and outgroups.

We could post these images at different stations around the room and ask students to work in small groups to examine each one of them, recording the group's responses to questions such as

- ♦ What are your first impressions of this person?
- ♦ What is there about the image that gives you these impressions?
- ♦ How well do you think you would get along with this person? Why do you think that?

After groups complete each station, we could then guide a whole class discussion focusing on questions such as

- ♦ What types of stereotypes have we experienced?
- ♦ How does it feel to be stereotyped?
- ♦ Why do we think that stereotypes are so powerful?
- ♦ What can we do to limit stereotyping?

In the second phase, we might ask students to complete their own individual examination of stereotypes with general directions such as

1. Identify a type of stereotyping you want to examine.
2. Find at least five images that relate to this type of stereotyping.
3. Study each of these images and describe the messages it sends and ways people might respond. Type your list under each image to begin your report.
4. Write a summary paper that describes:
    a. why you selected this type of stereotyping
    b. how you responded to these images
    c. what you learned about yourself in this process

Defining Your Identity

As students are navigating their personal morals, beliefs, and personalities, they are essentially building their identity. In this activity, you will prompt your students to think about the realities of perception and the misconceptions of identity.

1. Ask students to think about how the world (their peers, parents, coaches, teachers, for example) incorrectly labels or stereotypes them—a misconception of their identity. Some terms students may share include bully, nerd, dumb jock, boy-crazy, mean girl, and the like.
2. Now prompt students to write their negative label on one side of an index card with the definition and personal explanation on the back.
3. Once complete, have students think about who they truly see themselves to be. How do they want to be seen? Some adjectives students may choose are loving, hard-working, genuine, trustworthy, leader, and athletic.
4. Finally, ask students to write their new word on one side of an index card with the definition and explanation on the back.

This can be an extremely emotional activity for students, so gauge the temperature of your classroom and consider asking students to share the juxtaposition between their words only if they are comfortable doing so. Be certain to discuss the emphasis society may place on both words selected, linking this back to personal identity and the accuracy of whom we know ourselves to be versus how others might perceive us.

Let's turn to Madison for a personal story about the ways in which this activity impacted her high school students, and her.

I implemented this activity as a launch to a Problem Based Learning (PBL) experience centered on serving the homeless population in our community. Before we begin, note that this PBL spanned multiple classrooms from different schools, both a middle school and then my high school. These classes partnered to help address the problems associated with homelessness in our area. Before tackling the project, however, my co-teachers and I knew we needed to address the issue of stereotyping, so we encouraged our students to look deeper into how we often identify people incorrectly. With that in mind, we implemented the steps listed above in Defining your Identity, and one student's words have never left me.

When asked to choose the first word, the one that was a misconception of their personal identity, one student—quirky, all dressed in dark clothing, liked hard metal music, and often bullied—wrote MONSTER on his paper. My breath caught. I asked the student, "Why did you choose this word?" His response crushed me: "Because people see me as a monster. They make fun of me and say I am going to 'shoot up the school' when I would NEVER do that. I just like different things than other people, and I am different, but that doesn't mean I want to hurt anyone. I'm not a monster." Again, my teacher-heart ached, for I knew this student was just one of many trying to navigate the overwhelming landscape of adolescence.

Once we moved to the final steps of the activity where students choose, define, and explain the word they want the world to identify them as, I was eager to see which word that student chose. As I made my way through the classroom, I saw him writing TRUSTED on his paper. Wow. This misunderstood tenth grader's biggest desire was to be trusted. I thought I'd see if I couldn't make that happen, at least in my own classroom.

> *Due to the sensitivity of many students' words and explanations, we did not verbally discuss their descriptors as a class, but there was a clear shift in our classroom culture following this activity that day, one of acceptance and inclusion.*

References

Benson, P. L., Leffert, N., Scales, P. C., & Blyth, D. A. (1998). Beyond the "Village" Rhetoric: Creating Healthy Communities for Children and Adolescents. *Applied Developmental Science*, 2, 138–159.

Boaler, J. (2013, March). Ability and Mathematics: The Mindset Revolution that is Reshaping Education. *Forum*, 55(1), 143–152.

Canfield, J., & Wells, H.C. (1976). *100 Ways to Enhance Self-Concept in the Classroom*. Englewood Cliffs, NJ: Prentice-Hall.

Carlo, G., Padilla-Walker, L.M., & Nielson, M.G. (2015). Longitudinal Bidirectional Relations Between Adolescents' Sympathy and Prosocial Behavior. *Developmental Psychology*, 51, 1771. https://doi.org/10.1037/dev0000056

Crone, E. (2017). *The Adolescent Brain: Changes in Learning, Decision-Making, and Social Relations*. New York, NY: Routledge.

Dweck, C.S. (2008). *Mindsets and Math/Science Achievement*. New York, NY and Princeton, NJ: Carnegie Corporation of New York and the Institute for Advanced Study.

Dweck, C.S. (2010). Mindsets and Equitable Education. *Principal Leadership*, 10(5), 26–29.

Farrington, C.A., Roderick, M., Allensworth, E., Nagaoka, J., Keyes, T.S., Johnson, D.W., & Beechum, N.O. (2012). *Teaching Adolescents to Become Learners. The Role of Noncognitive Factors in Shaping School Performance: A Critical Literature Review*. Chicago: University of Chicago Consortium on Chicago School Research.

Filipello, P., Buzzai, C., Costa, S., Orecchio, S., & Sorrenti, L. (2020). Teaching Style and Academic Achievement: The Mediating Role of Learned Helplessness and Mastery Orientation. *Psychology in the Schools*, 57(1), 5–16.

Lee, Y.H., Heeter, C., Magerko, B., & Medler, B. (2012). Gaming Mindsets: Implicit Theories in Serious Game Learning. *Cyberpsychology, Behavior, and Social Networking*, 15(4), 190–194.

Nagaoka, J., Farrington, C.A., Ehrlich, S.B. & Heath, R.D. (2015). *Foundations for Young Adult Success: A Developmental Framework*. Chicago, IL: The University of Chicago Consortium on Chicago School Research.

Paluck, E.L., Shepherd, H., & Aronow, P.M. (2016). Changing Climates Of Conflict: A Social Network Experiment in 56 Schools. *Proceedings of the National Academy of Sciences*, 113(3), 566–571.

Pennsylvania State University. (2017) Issue Brief: *Promoting Social and Emotional Learning in the Middle and High School Years*. Pennsylvania State University. https://www.rwjf.org/socialemotionallearning

Quimby, D., Richards, M., Santiago, C.D., Scott, D., & Puvar, D. (2017). Positive Peer Association Among Black American Youth and the Roles of Ethnic Identity and Gender. *Journal of Research on Adolescence*, 28(3), 711–730.

Rivas-Drake, D., & Umaña-Taylor, A.J., (2019). How Do Youth Form Their Ideas about Ethnicity and Race? In D. Rivas-Drake and A. J. Umaña-Taylor, Eds., *Below the Surface: Talking with Teens about Race, Ethnicity, and Identity*. Princeton, NJ: Princeton University Press, 71–98.

Strahan, D., Hansen, K., Meyer, A., Buchanan, R., & Doherty, J. (2017). Integrating Mindset Interventions with Language Arts Instruction: An Exploratory Study with Seventh Grade Students. *RMLE Online*, 40(7), 1–15. DOI: 10.1080/19404476.2017.1349986

The Collaborative for Academic, Social, and Emotional Learning (CASEL). (2017). Core SEL Competencies. https://casel.org/core-competencies/

Tomlin, D. (2017). All in for Middle Level Education Month. http://www.amle.org/BrowsebyTopic/WhatsNew/WNDet.aspx?ArtMID=888&ArticleID=788

Van der Graaf, J., Carlo, G., Crocetti, E., Koot, H.M., & Branje S. (2017). Prosocial Behavior in Adolescence: Gender Differences in Development and Links with Empathy. *Journal of Youth and Adolescence*, 47(5), 1086–1099.

Wilson, T., Karimpour, R., & Rodkin, P. C. (2011). African American and European American Students' Peer Groups During Early Adolescence: Structure, Status, and Academic Achievement. *The Journal of Early Adolescence*, 31(1), 74–98.

6

Collaborating and Advocating
Supporting Teachers and Adolescents in Challenging Times

As discussed throughout this book, the fundamental premise of successfully teaching adolescent learners—really teaching them *well*—is that the better we understand our students, the better we can create caring connections with them, connections that draw them into learning as partners in the process. The research we have reported and the classroom narratives our teacher colleagues have shared demonstrate that successful teachers find ways to support their specific students, as individuals and as groups.

In our final chapter, we summarize essential insights from our research and shared narratives based on our Framework for Teaching Well with Adolescent Learners. We also link our work to the AMLE flagship publication *The Successful Middle School: This We Believe* (Bishop & Harrison, 2021), with its clear call to advocacy for all adolescents. Finally, we reach back into Ms. Hutchison's situation as an example of one way that a struggling teacher can find herself surrounded by a supportive school community to the great benefit of all.

As indicated in the diagram, teaching well begins with *understanding and supporting developmental changes* students are experiencing. This then guides teachers in *creating positive relationships with students to foster awareness of self and others*. Successful teachers draw

```
                    Understanding and supporting
                       developmental changes


                       TEACHING WELL WITH
                       ADOLESCENT LEARNERS


    Implementing                              Creating positive
    responsive                                relationships with
    teaching practices                        students that foster
    that extend connections                   awareness of self
    with academic concepts                    and others
                       Necessary conditions:
                     Classroom communities that
                    nurture trust and collaboration
```

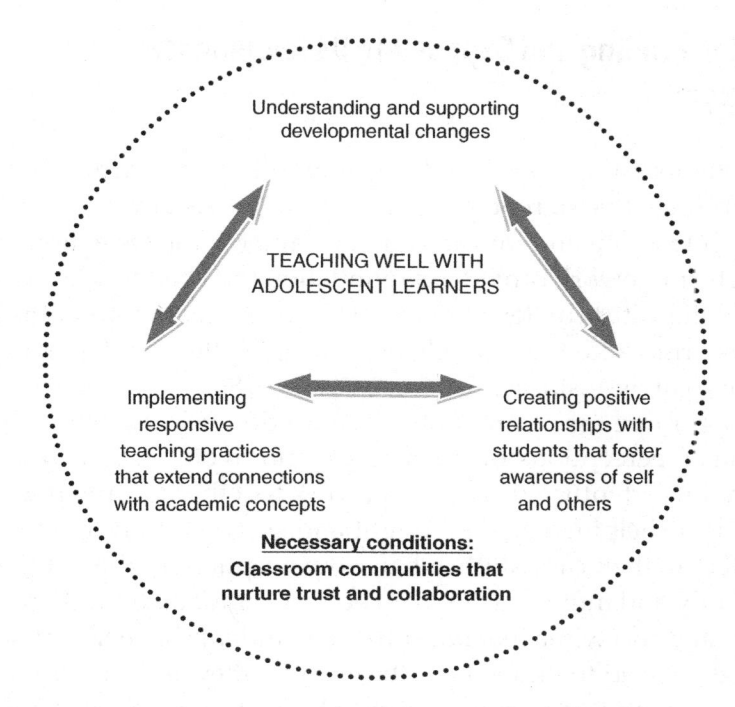

Figure 6.1 A framework for teaching well with adolescent learners

from research on good teaching and on the wisdom of practice to direct them in *implementing responsive teaching practices that extend connections with academic concepts*. An essential element of teaching well is *assuring the necessary conditions for a threshold of engagement: classroom communities that nurture trust and collaboration.*

The foundation for these dynamics is the process of observing students—really *seeing* and *hearing* them, that constant practice of studying students to learn more about them. By carefully observing what they say and do, successful teachers invite students to collaborate with them in learning more about who they are, what they care about, what they do well, and what types of conditions enable them to learn best. This interactive, ongoing process empowers teachers to

- understand and support developmental changes with individuals and groups
- keep a careful eye on relationships with and among students
- monitor progress toward academic connections

Understanding and Supporting Developmental Changes

Throughout this book, we have shown how teachers can combat the negative stereotyping of adolescents. As developed by the Search Institute and introduced in Chapter 1, the Developmental Assets framework provides a foundation for a better understanding of the nature of developmental changes, and the strengths students bring with them to school (Benson, Leffert, Scales, & Blyth, 1998; Search Institute, 2018a, 2018b, 2018c). Adolescents who possess more assets are more likely to do well in school, report stronger perceptions of themselves, and avoid risky behaviors. More importantly, educators can work together to strengthen assets, thus helping ensure a bright and successful future for each student in their care. With enhanced perceptions of the changes in the body and mind, teachers can be more empathetic and provide more support while making sure their students have the information they need to understand the changes they are experiencing.

These primary areas include physical and sexual development, intellectual and emotional growth, the development of a personal identity, and patterns of social and moral development. These four key dimensions, each detailed in an earlier chapter, are summarized here.

Patterns of Physical and Sexual Development

- ♦ The most visible phase of puberty typically begins in early adolescence, generally ages 9 to 11. Changes in hormones produce obvious "significant changes" in body parts, with girls entering puberty about one to two years before boys. While some of these physical changes are private, many are noticeable, such as hair growth, weight gain, and body odor.
- ♦ Adolescents progress through puberty at different rates of growth due to a multitude of influencers on the ignition and pace of puberty, such as environment, biological make-up, nutrition, and stress.

- Puberty also comes with social and emotional impact, especially for the students who develop outside the average window of time (both early and late pubertal developers). This serves as one example of the many ways in which one area of development influences another.
- While all adolescents are vulnerable during pubertal maturation, studies show there are biases and inequities in the treatment and perceptions of minority adolescents. A dangerous risk is adultification which occurs when adults treat Black adolescents as less innocent and more adult-like than their white peers.
- Home life, parental education, access to nutritional foods, and proximity to areas suitable for exercise all impact students' chances of being at risk for poor health, limited education, and a decreased quality of life. While we may not be able to impact life outside the school building, we should do what we can to provide nutritious food, knowledge about healthy eating, and opportunities for exercise.
- Adolescents need more sleep than adults do, with approximately nine hours of sleep per night optimal for the full physical, mental, and cognitive benefits of sleep. Neglecting this need for long periods can negatively impact growth and development.
- During adolescence, some bones finish forming, especially tailbones and kneecaps. These changes often contribute to feelings of discomfort in rigid physical settings, which then creates distraction. Educators can partially mitigate this within the instructional day by providing such things as flexible seating.

Patterns of Intellectual and Emotional Development
- Dramatic changes in brain activity occur between ages 11 and 15. During this period of development, neural pruning occurs at a rapid rate, creating intense "neuroplasticity," changes in neural connections that accompany learning experiences.

- Changes to the cortical regions of the brain come more slowly, so cognitive control and self-regulation develop more gradually. Together these functions of the prefrontal cortex enable skills of *executive function*: selective attention, decision-making, voluntary responsive inhibition, and working memory. Adolescents may experience unpredictable fluctuations in reasoning processes. Until executive functions mature, planning may be a challenge, especially in different contexts.
- Across the period of adolescence, maturation occurs in the prefrontal cortex and enables dramatic growth in executive functioning, cognitive control, and impulse management. Important changes in thinking include
  - greater capacity for memory recall and retention
  - more sophisticated goal selection
  - stronger working memory
  - greater capacity for self-regulation of affect and behavior
  - more accurate use of evidence to draw conclusions
- The neuroplasticity of developing brains and the increasing abilities of metacognition enable growing powers of representational thought.
  - As processing grows more sophisticated, adolescents become increasingly aware of how they think and feel.
  - A growing capacity for metacognition is especially important in making sense of the emotional aspects of thinking.
  - Adolescents are learning to recognize impressions, intuitions, and intentions.
- Emotional development is a complex, negotiated process. Positive experiences affirm positive perceptions and soften negative ones. Negative experiences reinforce doubts and weaken confidence. Together, these interactions shape perceptions of identity, which then influence the next set of interactions. At each moment, feelings and understandings intertwine and become inseparable as they create thoughts.
- Growing powers of metacognition make possible a greater awareness of personal interests and passions. Students often find activities that engage them intensely, such as music, art, sports, video games, and reading.

Development of Personal Identity

- Throughout childhood and into adolescence, identity becomes increasingly defined. "Who am I?" and "How do I relate to others?" become pressing questions.
- Identity is an emerging reflection of values, beliefs, and aspirations, constructed and reconstructed over time and experience, shaped by multiple factors that include family, culture, peers, and media.
- Adolescents develop a more resilient sense of self as they interact with the people around them to negotiate negative life experiences.
- Adolescents become more aware of things about themselves that they like and, perhaps, things about themselves they wish they could change. As a result, students often explore different identities, think about themselves in reference to peers and media, and choose to identify with peers with whom they feel they belong.
- Adolescents are actively engaged in sense-making. They try on new identities, try out new behaviors, and make decisions about who they are and whom they want to become. Schools play a vital role in this positive identity development, with classroom environments becoming proving grounds in many aspects.
- As an integrative construct, Ethnic and Racial Identity (ERI) encompasses students' beliefs about their group and how their ethnicity and race become a central aspect of their self-definition. General processes of identity development—exploring one's sense of self, interpreting messages from others, engaging in social comparisons—characterize the development of ethnic and racial identities.
- Increasing attention to issues of gender in recent years makes the search for identity more visible and provides more opportunities for an open exploration of gender than in years past.
- Peer dynamics greatly influence the negotiation of all aspects of identity.

Patterns of Social and Moral Development

- As a general pattern, concerns about social status and popularity become more pronounced in adolescence.
- Positive peer association results in higher levels of self-esteem and school connectedness.
- The formation of friendships is a complex process. Successful friendships require abilities to recognize emotions in others, establish a place within a group, deal with feelings of acceptance and rejection, and consider the perspectives of others.
- Perceptions of academic competence are shaped by social comparison in the same ways as other aspects of identity.
- Mindsets contribute to broader learning dispositions and academic behaviors. Students with a history of success engage with learning activities, pay attention, participate in class, and complete homework. These behaviors become habits for them, enabling the academic perseverance needed to accomplish challenging tasks.
- Developing strong academic mindsets enhances a more resilient sense of self, extending the development of personal power, self-esteem, sense of purpose, and positive views of personal future. Negative mindsets, in contrast, may lead to a sense of learned helplessness.
- Students who engage most with new social situations and academic tasks are those who 1) learn to reflect more thoughtfully about their own thinking and their own engagement and 2) begin to feel a sense of ownership for their own learning.
- Adolescents strengthen concepts of right and wrong and develop notions of justice in ways that are interactive and contextual.
- Empathy is the heart of moral behavior.
  - A key aspect in the development of empathy is prosocial behavior, which generally is defined as voluntary behavior intended to benefit others.
  - Such behavior is clearly a developmental asset, strongly associated with high self-esteem, academic success, and positive social relationships.

- During adolescence, we see a gradual transition from perspectives dominated by self toward perspectives that include others. Mature perspective-taking becomes possible in later adolescence.
- Essential skills include projecting situations into the future, seeing different angles, and putting things into perspective. These skills enable a sense of autonomy – knowing that one can make independent decisions and take care of oneself.
- Growing powers of reasoning enable reflection, which strengthens values.

♦ While these general patterns describe changes for groups, individuals vary greatly in the extent to which they make sense of social situations and demonstrate moral reasoning.

Understanding the specifics of adolescent development will allow teachers to better support changes like the ones summarized here, establish positive relationships, and implement responsive teaching practices in their classrooms and schools.

Creating Positive Relationships

As we emphasized in Chapter 1, researchers have concluded, "Nothing has more impact in the life of a child than positive relationships" (Roehlkepartain et al., 2017, p. 3). The five critical elements of The Relationships First Framework provide a strong foundation for success

- ♦ Expressing care—showing that students matter
- ♦ Challenging growth—pushing students to keep getting better
- ♦ Providing support—helping students complete tasks and achieve goals
- ♦ Sharing power—treating students with respect and giving them a say
- ♦ Expanding possibilities—connecting students with people and places that broaden their horizons

(p. 4)

Figure 6.2 Gaining confidence

A positive and nurturing school context is critical for providing these daily opportunities for students, as peer norms become especially influential, and students must have the chance to explore who they are and where they belong in a safe space. The most impacting educators demonstrate authentic caring, showing they respect students as individuals, understand and embrace their cultural backgrounds, and address their strengths in academic lessons. These caring teachers support the development of a student's more resilient sense of self. As a result, their classrooms are places where adolescents can explore personal identities, learn to interpret messages from others with greater confidence and sophistication, and engage in supportive social comparisons.

Implementing Responsive Teaching Practices

Once these relationships have been ensured, students tend to embrace academic opportunities more readily, including the responsive teaching practices that lead to authentic learning. These instructional experiences are certainly critical factors in the development of a deeper understanding of content and self. Ideas develop as students first learn individual concepts, then connect those concepts into relationships, and finally generate their own creative applications of those concepts. With the right support, adolescents' capacity for flexibility and adaptability can foster deep learning, complex problem-solving skills, and creativity.

Experienced teachers know that in order to gain academic confidence, students need a delicate combination of encouragement and coaching, a process similar to learning to walk—a small-steps approach to learning. This scaffolding, including appropriate monitoring and reteaching, can lead to individualized classroom success for students, ensuring a healthy growth mindset. These teachers know that deeper learning is possible through their use of perceptive analytical skills, which allows them to understand better how their students' thinking grows more sophisticated as they process surface-level information and generate deeper connections. This, in turn, helps successful teachers plan lessons that scaffold instruction. Finally, to ensure effective application, they tailor their plans to students' interests and emotions, as well as to their academic knowledge and skills. This, as a result, assures a classroom that is based in great measure on trust and collaboration.

Assuring the Necessary Conditions for a Threshold of Engagement: Classroom Communities That Nurture Trust and Collaboration

Trusting a caring teacher dramatically increases the odds that students will take chances and invest effort in new challenges. Trusting relationships constitute a threshold of action, a point beyond which meaningful learning can occur. Adolescents negotiate physical changes, mental growth, and life experiences to achieve a more resilient sense of self, and they depend on safe classroom and school spaces to allow this mature growth. They make sense of the messages they receive and their encounters with the world to acquire confident views of their identities, gain social and academic competence, and establish stronger moral and ethical systems. When teachers demonstrate authentic caring, they accelerate positive development by showing they respect students as individuals, understanding and embracing their cultural backgrounds, and addressing their strengths in lessons.

The research we have reviewed and the narratives shared by our teacher colleagues together demonstrate the powerful influence that dedicated and mindful educators offer when they invest fully in their students. When educators show students they respect them, adolescents recognize that their teachers care for them, and they reciprocate that investment.

Understanding Challenges to Positive Youth Development

Throughout this book, we have emphasized the potential of adolescence as a time for powerful growth and learning. We have described ways that students enter grade six and move through middle school and high school on their journey toward adulthood. We have underscored the value of understanding these changes from the perspective of the Developmental Assets framework (The Search Institute, 1997, 2018a, 2018b, 2018c). Reviews of research, illustrations applying that research, and narratives from classroom teachers have merged to demonstrate ways that middle school and high school teachers play a critical role in nurturing positive development. With support from teachers, students strengthen their internal assets. They increase their commitment to learning, reinforce positive values, improve their social competencies, and consolidate their sense of identity. Consequently, when they have spent time in good schools, adolescents go on to the next level with more assets than they had when they began. The notion of the resilient individual who can overcome obstacles and achieve healthy adulthood on his or her own is misleading. Context matters tremendously.

As we noted in the first chapter, we have drawn guidance for our text from the most recent version of AMLE's foundational position volume, *The Successful Middle School: This We Believe* (2021) by Penny Bishop and Lisa Harrison. This guidance has been bittersweet. On the one hand, the authors document, in detail, practices that provide engaging, supportive, and inspiring educational experiences. On the other, we agree that these experiences are not nearly as available to all adolescents as they should be. "Research is clear that not all youth have the same access to responsive middle schools that lay a foundation for success. Learners from historically marginalized groups disproportionally suffer the harmful consequences of bias, discrimination, and systemic oppression" (Bishop & Harrison, 2021, p. 4).

These inequities affect health and development as well as education. The authors of *The Promise of Adolescence: Realizing Opportunity for All Youth* (National Academies of Sciences, Engineering, and Medicine, 2019) document the profound impacts of poverty and marginalization.

> More than 9 million children and youth (ages 0 to 18) in the United States live in households with incomes below the poverty level, and rates of child poverty are highest for Black, Latinx, and American Indian and Alaska Native youth. For adolescents, growing up in poverty is associated with worse physical and mental health, as well as higher prevalence of risky behaviors and delinquency.
> (p.4)

Other recent reports reinforce these reminders about the urgency of taking better care of our young people. In a study with more than 15,000 high school students from 125 schools, researchers found that

- Nearly 6% of the female participants and 11% of the male participants revealed they had been involved in a physical fight at school.
- 22% of females and 16% of males revealed that they had experienced bullying.

- 10% of males and 8% of females had been threatened or injured with a weapon in the school setting.
- 11% of females reported being a victim of sexual dating violence.
- Approximately 30% reported encountering feelings of sadness or hopelessness.

    (Kim, Sanders, Makubuya, & Yu, 2020, p. 731)

Students exposed to violence have a higher risk of depression, emotional difficulties, and inhibited academic achievement.

> Feeling safe in school is an important aspect of school connection, and school connectedness is increasingly understood to play an important role in student success. Students' positive perceptions of safety at their school were associated with higher academic achievement in reading and math, suggesting that students preoccupied with safety concerns are less able to focus on academics.
>
>   (Kim, Sanders, Makubuya, & Yu, 2020, p. 726)

Researchers concluded:

> The results of this study provide important insight into the complex relationships between experiencing school violence, perceptions of school safety, sadness and hopelessness and their relationship to academic performance. Knowing the type of school violence that is experienced, its ramifications, and recognizing that males and females may be impacted differently is vital when designing and implementing interventions necessary in maintaining overall wellbeing in schools.
>
>   (Kim, Sanders, Makubuya, & Yu, 2020, p. 740)

Faced with these challenges, we join Bishop and Harrison (2021) in calling for stronger advocacy for change.

> To achieve truly responsive middle schools, educators recognize these inequities and implement practices and policies to redress and disrupt them. These practices and

> policies justly ensure that each student feels socially connected and valued, becomes competent and skilled, and develops independence and responsibility.
>
> (p. 4)

As teachers, we find it natural to advocate for equity defined broadly. We understand the impact of poverty on children. Access to good nutrition, healthcare, quality childcare, and print and digital educational resources all make a substantial difference in the external assets children bring with them to school. When researchers examine the results of educational assessments, poverty is always the most significant variable.

To advocate for adolescents at the ground level—within our schools and classrooms—can feel daunting and overwhelming. We see the impact of poverty and marginalization daily. We know which of our students are the have-nots, which are the have-a-lots, and which sometimes have and sometimes do not have. We know which students are most visible, whose voices are heard, and whose voices are often silent or ignored. We watch and listen as these differences play out in the hallways, in the lunchroom, and, often, in our assessments. We do what we can to make our classrooms safe and inviting spaces. To advocate beyond our classroom walls, we need support. Collaboration with colleagues and other caring adults is our best hope.

The Successful Middle School: This We Believe (Bishop & Harrison, 2021) provides a powerful framework for transformative collaboration. Organized by five essential attributes and 18 specific characteristics, this framework defines successful middle level schooling.

> These descriptors, rooted in research and experience, provide a framework for creating the learning environments and opportunities that all young adolescents deserve. One profound lesson learned in more than 60 years of active middle school practice, research, and advocacy is that these attributes and characteristics are interdependent and need to be implemented in concert.
>
> (p. 6)

Figure 6.3 Teaching well with a spirit of adventure

Our Framework for Teaching Well with Adolescent Learners substantiates this emphasis on comprehensive, integrative approaches to teaching and expands the need to include all young adolescents in grades six through ten, for their developmental vulnerability extends to the early years of high school as well. The connective tissue of such approaches is a commitment to deeply understanding students and collaborating with them as groups and individuals. Developing these responsive practices to teach well to adolescent learners requires flexibility, deep knowledge, growing wisdom, and a spirit of adventure.

In this text, we have highlighted examples of responsive practices that illustrate the five Essential Attributes of *The Successful Middle School*. Table 6.1 provides a few of these examples.

The developmental changes adolescent learners must navigate are widely considered the most significant in the life span from conception to about age 21. As they change physically, sexually and intellectually, it is critical that those adults to whom they have been entrusted help them grow in healthy emotional, social, and moral ways, as well. As Ms. Hutchison eventually came to realize, their future depends on that.

Table 6.1 Teaching Well with Adolescent Learners: Connections with *The Successful Middle School: This We Believe*

Essential Attributes of *The Successful Middle School (p. 8)* AMLE affirms that an education for young adolescents must be:	Examples and illustrations from *Teaching Well with Adolescent Learners: Responding to Developmental Changes in Middle School and High School*
Responsive Using the distinctive nature and identities of young adolescents as the foundation upon which all decisions about school are made.	♦ Using the Developmental Assets framework (Chapter 1) ♦ Kayla's Story (Chapter 2) ♦ Flexible seating (Chapter 2)
Challenging Cultivating high expectations and advancing learning for every member of the school community.	♦ Assessing levels of understanding in a progression from surface to deep (Chapter 3) ♦ Expanded concept maps (Chapter 3)
Empowering Facilitating environments in which students take responsibility for their own learning and contribute positively to the world around them.	♦ Digging Deeper than the Surface is Always Worth It (Chapter 1) ♦ Constant Conversation and Guidance Activity: An Open Dialogue Centered on Trust (Chapter 2) ♦ Encouraging Competency – Anthony's Case (Chapter 5)
Equitable Providing socially just learning opportunities and environments for every student.	♦ Authentic caring (respecting students as individuals, understanding and embracing their racial and cultural backgrounds, and addressing their strengths in lessons (Chapter 4, Chapter 5) ♦ Supporting Charlotte and her Classmates (Chapter 4) ♦ Exploring images and stereotypes (Chapter 4, Chapter 5)
Engaging Fostering a learning atmosphere that is relevant, participatory, and motivating for all adolescents.	♦ Analysis of a Science Unit (Chapter 3) ♦ Michael's case study (Chapter 3) ♦ A small steps approach to social and academic competence (Chapter 5)

The Story of Ms. Hutchison Revisited

Let us summarize our scenario, then fast forward a bit as we return to the story of Ms. Hutchison, our teacher in Chapter 1, who, like many new to the profession, entered joyfully but quickly became overwhelmed by the reality of what she encountered. As you will recall, we left her disillusioned not only with her ninth-grade classroom but also with the out-of-touch graduate course that her licensure program required, and she had eventually contacted her former supervisor inquiring about a position on another research team. Determined to leave her classroom behind permanently, Ms. Hutchison looked forward to ending both the graduate semester and her short-lived teaching career.

As often happens, however, her former position was no longer available, and her supervisor did not anticipate anything opening up for at least another six months or so, though he felt like the job would then be hers should she want it. Because she knew she needed employment and immediate jobs seemed scarce in her field, she reconciled herself to returning to her classroom in the fall, though she latched onto the idea that she could always leave in late December, given the tentative grant position they had discussed. Discouraged on that early June afternoon, she began to clean her classroom and make a few summer plans, but she stopped short of sharing her intention to return eventually to fieldwork.

As a Beginning Teacher (BT), Ms. Hutchison planned for two year-end events. The first was the obligatory BT conversation with her administrator, one where she would discuss her annual academic goals and progress toward them and, based on that, set professional goals for the coming year. Despite her best intentions to remain neutral, her frustrations must have lived on her face because her principal stopped her mid-report and offered a few suggestions based on his ongoing observations of Ms. Hutchison's teaching and her interactions with faculty.

"Let's talk candidly," he began, and it seemed this broke through the ice, cracking Ms. Hutchison's resolve to remain neutral, get this meeting done, and simply escape into summer. "I've watched you closely over the last few months, and it's been obvious that you've become increasingly unhappy with both your classroom and yourself. You've amplified your office referrals, silenced yourself in BT meetings, missed a scheduled conversation with your mentor, and I have just received an emailed complaint from a parent about your spiraling management issues. I am really concerned about all of this. You opened the school year enthused and patient, but both of those have been in short supply as the year, and especially this spring semester, have moved forward. Talk to me. What's going on, and how can we support you—how can I help you work through this so that summer gives you back your teaching energy?"

She began a hesitant response but then remembered the possibility of leaving in late December and knew she had nothing to lose. "What the heck," she thought, and she told him everything, from the unrealistic graduate course to the overwhelming workload and her struggles with maintaining any semblance of classroom order and effectiveness. The conversation that ensued was just that: a true discussion with back-and-forth ideas and implications for the summer and fall ahead. Ms. Hutchison left that afternoon feeling lighter than she had in months, and, on reflection, found that she felt almost as excited as she had in those early days of fall. At last, she had a sympathetic ear tuned to her and some concrete suggestions from an expert. Resigned to return the upcoming fall yet resolved to try a few select ideas, she headed back to her classroom, grabbed her tablet, and began to log in the best of his suggestions, gleaning them for rank order.

The second event on her calendar, the faculty meeting, was scheduled for the end of the week and was promoted as a debriefing on the academic year. The principal opened with the expected reports on assessment scores, progress made toward the School Improvement Plan goals, and an overview of a few new state bills and mandates that could potentially affect the next academic year. Ms. Hutchison had expected the meeting to be information-delivery-and-overload and was surprised when he asked teachers to cluster themselves around the cafeteria tables based on their years of teaching experience. The activity that followed both intrigued and excited her, for she immediately saw it as a model for her own instruction, all the while feeling certain that it was driven by the earlier BT discussion she had with him—she felt valued and energized all over again.

He challenged the faculty to think within their groups according to their years of teaching:

> I want you to work as a team and share your collective wisdom with each other, which we'll later share with the whole faculty. Brainstorm and record on chart paper your discussion notes based on these directives:
>
> ♦ If you are a BT with less than three full years' experience, what are the things you have conquered—not mastered, conquered—this year, and what are the five things you need immediate help with now over the summer months?
> ♦ If you have taught for four to ten complete years, what do you know now that you wish you had known then? Record the highlights of that discussion.
> ♦ And finally, if you have taught longer than ten years, ask yourselves what the best advice is for a new teacher and list ten non-negotiables based on that advice.

After a period of brainstorming, recording, and then sharing, the faculty left for summer with many of them, Ms. Hutchison included, snapping pictures of the wall charts—what a goldmine of information! It was all there, the collective early-years' frustrations, the mid-years' growth into expertise, and finally the deep wisdom that comes from blending knowledge with varied and repeated experience. She could not wait to begin trying some of this! She suddenly found herself out of the isolation of her classroom and into the feeling of collegiality that she realized she had been unconsciously missing, or perhaps even avoiding.

Let us step aside and examine some of those suggestions under the spotlight of what we know about good teaching. As has been underscored in our *Framework for Teaching Well with Adolescent Learners*, strong and effective teachers develop positive relationships with all students—every single one—relationships based on a deep understanding of and support for the developmental changes that hallmark the early years of adolescence, ages 11 to 15, approximately. From there, they use that knowledge to implement responsive teaching practices that guide a rich knowledge of key academic concepts, all grounded in a classroom climate of trust and collaboration. That description ensures the evolution of a learner who is ready for schooling and embraces the opportunities it provides, growing into the young adult who is then ready to meet successfully the challenging world outside the controlled environment of school.

In Ms. Hutchison's story, her colleague's advice validates this thinking. (*Note*: in reality, this advice was gathered from approximately 60 experienced middle and high school teachers and is clustered here under common categories that emerged from that data). Let us close with some of their best suggestions for your consideration and implementation.

- **Build your community early and tap it often.**

Teaching was never meant to be done in isolation. Lean into the positive aspects of schooling. What is out there that can help you, and whom does that involve? For example, and no matter your experience level, start investigating sound instructional practices during those first workdays. Ask your colleagues. Brainstorm within your interdisciplinary team, your Professional Learning Communities, content departments, grade-level colleagues, and with your mentor or site facilitator. Ask to observe experienced teachers who are solid with a strategy or a piece of the mandated curriculum that you are struggling with or unsure of. Search your college texts and the internet, and ask your colleagues for their book recommendations and favorite, proven websites. Email former professors who were especially effective in the ways of strong teaching and invite them to observe you and dialogue about multiple aspects of your classroom. Recognize early on that not every student will engage with every lesson, every activity, or sometimes even any of them—do your best and keep digging for answers.

Ask your assigned mentor to lunch during the opening workdays and bring your calendar with the expectation of scheduling regular meetings and observations. Don't have a mentor? Request one or seek one out yourself. You are a mentor? Then reverse that table and know how deeply your BT depends on your input for his or her success. Get to know the office administrative assistants, custodial staff, and support teachers like the technology and media specialists. Go to professional development opportunities, and ask your administration to add topics that you and your colleagues need that are not scheduled. Read books that address a concern you have or listen to them via an audible book club as you drive to and from school or as you enjoy an afternoon workout or a walk around your neighborhood. Keep a journal and review it often for personal behavior patterns and idea notes, including snapshots of everything from bulletin boards to desk arrangements. Stay inquisitive.

Find your voice and use it, remembering all the while that you, too, are an important part of someone else's growing community. Reflect daily on your successes and identify your struggles and concerns, adding those notes to your journal. You are building a support system for yourself—go to the community to learn; there is wisdom in practice and that is well represented in every school. This will be critical for your classroom effectiveness and mental well-being. Do good every day. Tap your total system for many things, and, above all, as in the case of Ms. Hutchison, be honest with your administration. That group of school leaders can be a phenomenal asset if you persist in your quest for support, but they cannot help you if they do not know there's a problem.

◆ **Realize that classroom management begins before the students arrive.**

Teachers often think of management as synonymous with controlling student behavior, but that is only a part of what this umbrella term encompasses. Developing solid, purposeful systems promotes a sense of independence among your classes and frees you to focus on the needs of individual students and effective teaching practices.

For example, can you articulate the type of classroom you want to create? How do you want students to interact within that space? How can you ensure that it is a safe place for trying new things and making mistakes—the heart of a learning environment? How do parents fit in? What are your simple routines for assigning homework and then collecting it, including handling make-up work for students who are absent? How will you keep track of those assignments and grades, and how will you ensure that your students are fully aware of their scores? Do you know for sure that each child comes from a well-equipped and supportive home environment? That answer alone can dramatically increase your capacity for individualizing your assignments and management expectations. What is your discipline plan for misbehavior, and how will you enforce that? Do you know the root cause of that misbehavior? How do you praise for a job well done, and is praise more plentiful than punishment? How public are you with all this? (The unspoken code of adolescence requires students to save face when addressed in embarrassing ways, so do not embarrass them.) Are you proactive rather than reactive? Do you head-rehearse potential scenarios so that you can vicariously practice your response to them?

If you are new to the profession, observe successful classroom managers with about five years' experience (they remember what it is like to stand where you are). During those observations, make notes about their classroom routines and student relationships; ask that teacher who he or she thinks is a successful classroom manager and then spiral additional observations from there, asking each in turn for another name, gradually moving to more experienced colleagues. Ask your students for advice (a great, relevant writing assignment!). How does all that tie into the school's expectations and mission? Are your rules clearly stated, enforceable, and fully understood by every student? How do you know this? Do parents know your expectations? Does your administration know them and approve? (They cannot support you if they do not know what you are doing.) Do you have appropriate consequences that are consistent and fair? Do students have opportunities to reflect on the choices they make and suggest authentic consequences for those decisions? Do you keep accurate, dated records as evidence to share with a student as needed—you will find patterns in that evidence that will provide important clues to a child's individual needs. Also, try to avoid office referrals unless it is a serious infraction—every time you send a student out of your classroom, in their eyes, you turn your authority over to someone else, diminishing your own.

And perhaps most important: do your students know you care about them? How is that obvious without you having to say it? Adolescents will often feed off your emotions, so the answers to these questions, coupled with a calm demeanor and a smile from you, can shift the power away from the misbehaving or emotionally reactive student and back to you. This, in turn, will bring you a step closer to your goal of growing healthy, successful, self-disciplined young adults who can navigate the world outside of your classroom.

- ◆ **Learn about every student and his/her unique needs and strengths. Students are an asset, not a deficit; respect that.**

That often-referenced saying about students not caring what you know until they know you care is likely more relevant today than ever before as we navigate one world crisis after another. Students are fearful, and, for many, we are both their shield against a frightening world and their hope for a successful place within it. They crave consistently positive, dependable adults in their lives. Get to know them, explore their world, and situate yourself within it as a point of reflection, all the while examining your classroom atmosphere, instructional strategies, and management plan for relevance and, when needed, revision.

Central Cabarrus High School (Concord, NC) teacher Ashley Eyer cautions, "Remind yourself every day that, for the majority of the students you teach, your content is not their passion. Your class is merely a stepping-stone toward them achieving a bigger dream like graduation, college, a family, or the perfect job. As teachers, we climbed all of our stepping-stones to get to these kids; they *are* our bigger dream. Do not hold their lack of interest against them."

So how do we determine their interests? There are many avenues to choose from; for example, talk to them in the hallways and the cafeteria—a much more holistic view of their lives than responsibility for a content area. Read realistic adolescent fiction yourself as a way to explore the teenage world vicariously. Watch the television shows and movies they enjoy. Play the video games they report are best and listen to their music. Consider their media exposure. How would all that influence you if you were their age and regularly engaged in those genres? Attend after-school events and make sure they see you there—and if you say you will be there, be there; they will watch for you.

Occasionally ask them to do two-minute fast writes on index cards based on relevant questions that you have for them, like some of these: how important is school? How did the global pandemic affect your family? What do you think about school safety (or perhaps another event) and its impact on your family? How can we better address that sort of major concern here in our school and in this classroom? What traits do you value in a friend, and which of those traits do you need to work on yourself? Which parts of school do you consider most important to your future and which seem the least important? What advice do you have for me as your teacher? What is working in our classroom for you and what is not?

Describe the most effective teacher you have ever had—what did she or he do that was great? Keep yourself open to what you hear and see and adjust your thinking based on your students' advice and wisdom.

Our friend and mentor William Purkey teaches us that school should be the most inviting place in town, a place that brings a child in every day because there is something going on there that she or he does not want to miss: maybe it is you, perhaps it is the topic you are currently teaching, maybe it is the provided breakfast and lunch. It could be an art class or a sports team, or a chance to go to the media center. Perhaps for the ADHD child, it is the recognition that movement is critical; for the ADD child it could be that you privately rather than publicly redirect when that attention span lags. Maybe it is simply having a friend.

Regardless, find the Why and use that to invite each student in to learn and grow and be him or herself without judgment. That in itself can be the key to motivating every teenager to do his or her best for you—a teacher they respect and want to do well for. Have fun, enjoy your work, talk to them, learn from them, be approachable, and you will find that the classroom invites you in as much as it does your students. (For additional information on Invitational Education, see Purkey, W. W., Novak, J. M., & Fretz, J. R. [2020]. *Developing Inviting Schools: A Beneficial Framework for Teaching and Leading*. New York, NY: Teachers College Press.)

♦ **Be realistic. You are not Superman or Wonder Woman.**

If only Ms. Hutchison had known this from the first day of that first semester in her classroom. We expect so much of ourselves as teachers—true, we are that shield against the world, but shields are crafted of multiple layers; when combined, these layers produce a protection that appears invincible. In reality, however, a shield is only as strong as the combination of each layer, requiring regular maintenance to ensure the user's safety. Teachers often fail to recognize this and put their own needs aside for the immediacy of the classroom, morphing those needs into personal expectations for excellence that can be unrealistic and, as in the case of Ms. Hutchison, damaging enough to dash dreams, often leaving teachers depleted. How do we stand strong against this possibility, keeping all the layers of our personal shields intact?

The 60 middle and high school teachers who offered their advice in real-time commented on this balancing act, offering these suggestions:

Have clearly defined, realistic goals and make concrete plans for reaching them. Praise yourself for the progress made. North Stanly High School (New London, NC) teacher Chris Brown notes that "Comics have a phrase they use, 'Sucking the energy out of the room,' which they apply to a lackluster comic who is bombing and leaving the audience in a sleepy mood for the next comic. I've been that guy occasionally, as we all have." Sometimes we suck the energy out, sometimes our students do, sometimes it's the school or the district itself, sometimes it's politics or pandemics, but the reality is that it happens, and we need to deal with it, put it into perspective, and move forward. View everything as a learning experience. Try to leave your work at work, even if it means you must stay on campus longer after the teaching day ends, and, if you hold a second job, try to designate only a portion of your weekend for school planning and grading. All this may feel and actually be impossible your first year and maybe two, but look to the years following those and plan for them by keeping notes on each lesson and strategy, carefully recording what worked and what needs revision the next time around. It really does get easier when you keep the long view in front of you.

And how did Ms. Hutchison react to all this advice? She thoughtfully examined the list she created from her snapshots, highlighting and prioritizing the things she found most relevant to her for immediate implementation. There was certainly a trove of information to consider, and she carefully tucked the list into a ready file for continued reflection—a guide for her to rely on for the months ahead and to discuss with her colleagues. She felt empowered again from the value she found in the activity, the personal voice that she had been emboldened to express, and the potential for a better semester ahead.

Fortunately, our story of Ms. Hutchison does not end there. She spent a few extra days organizing her classroom, notes, and ideas before heading out for summer, and she returned in the fall to find that not only was her perspective more grounded but also the school's. As it turns out, her principal spent much of the summer reading books on contemporary issues that were prevalent in the school and community, like racial inequity, poverty, and factors influencing identity development among their teens. In addition, he read a text on early adolescent development that she recommended to him from her summer course, and together they planned professional development based on that reading, as her principal quickly realized that this stage in the life span was much different from the later adolescent years that the school had always focused on. As a result, part of the new year's mantra was the word *Stretch*, for the faculty agreed that it was only by tearing down boundaries and delving into what they knew least about that they could change their practice and classrooms into places of invitation, engagement, trust, and productive learning.

With her plans for grant-sponsored fieldwork now tucked into a far distant place, Ms. Hutchison found her fall classroom a shelter for acceptance and purposeful learning, one that she thrived in as much as her students. "I might not be able to change the world," she thought, "but I'm feeling pretty confident I can impact it in a mighty way for the kids who join me in my classroom every day."

References

Benson, P.L., Leffert, N., Scales, P.C., & Blyth, D.A. (1998). Beyond the "Village" Rhetoric: Creating Healthy Communities for Children and Adolescents. *Applied Developmental Science*, 2, 138–159.

Bishop, P., & Harrison, L. (2021). *The Successful Middle School: This We Believe*. Columbus, OH: The Association for Middle Level Education.

Kim, Y., K., Sanders, J. E., Makubuya, T., & Yu, M. (2020). Risk Factors of Academic Performance: Experiences of School Violence, School Safety Concerns, and Depression by Gender. *Child & Youth Care Forum*, 49, 725–742. https://doi.org/10.1007/s10566- 020-09552-7

National Academies of Sciences, Engineering, and Medicine. (2019). *The Promise of Adolescence: Realizing Opportunity for All Youth*. Washington, DC: The National Academies Press. https://doi.org/10.17226/25388

Roehlkepartain, E., Pekel, K., Syvertsen, A., Sethi, J., Sullivan, T., & Scales, P. (2017).

Relationships First: Creating Connections That Help Young People Thrive. Minneapolis, MN: Search Institute. Retrieved from http://page.search-institute.org/relationships-first5

Purkey, W. W., Novak, J. M., & Fretz, J. R. (2020). *Developing Inviting Schools: A Beneficial Framework for Teaching and Leading*. New York, NY: Teachers College Press.

Search Institute. (2003). Boosting Student Achievement: New Research on the Power of Developmental Assets. *Search Institute Insights & Evidence*, 1, 1.

Search Institute. (2018a). *Data Sheet: Developmental Assets among U.S. Youth: 2018 Update*. https://www.search-institute.org/wp-content/uploads/2018/01/DataSheet-Assets-x-Gender-2018-update.pdf

Search Institute. (2018b). *Data Sheet: Developmental Assets among U.S. Youth: 2018 Update*. https://www.search-institute.org/wp-content/uploads/2018/01/DataSheet-Assets-x-Race-Ethnicity-2018-update.pdf

Search Institute. (2018c). *Data Sheet: Developmental Assets among U.S. Youth: 2018 Update*. https://www.search-institute.org/wp-content/uploads/2018/01/DataSheet-Assets-x-LGBT-2018-update.pdf

Index

Note: **Bold** page numbers refer to tables; *italic* page numbers refer to figures.

abstract reasoning 76, 78–81
academic competence 153–157, 169, 185; activities for understanding students 170–173; connections among students' thoughts and actions 155–157; perceptions of 153, 181; "poker chip theory" of self-concept 154; role of student's mindsets 154–155, 157; small steps approach 159–161; social comparisons 153–154; *see also* social competence
academic confidence 184
academic mindsets 157, 182
academic motivation 20
acceptability, perceptions of 52
achievement motivation **15**, 16
acting white, avoiding accusations of 127–128
adolescent development: pattern of 19; research on 11–19; teaching in synchronization with 3–6
adolescents/adolescence 12, 13, 165, 177; brain growth during 69–71; celebrating teamwork *152*; changes in relationship to physical surroundings 58–61; conversation and guidance for 62–65; feelings of discomfort during 179; gaining confidence *184*; importance of sleep 179; learning from own experiences 102; needs of 3–4; as "positive window of opportunity" 23; progress through puberty 178; promotive factors for 112, 114; resilient sense of self 180; self-awareness 160, 161–162; self-understandings 117; sense-making 181; things about themselves 180–181; understanding changes during puberty 43–50

adultification of students of color 50–51, 178
adult relationships **14**, 17
adult role models **14**
agency 160, 161–162
analytical skills, perceptive 185
Anderson, M. 120
"App Generation" 119
Aronow, P. M. 150
Asheville City Schools 29
Association for Middle Level Education (AMLE) 3, 4, 6
attention 71; emotions shaping 68; to issues of gender 129, 181; selective 70, 179; on social and ethical dimensions 10; to social status 159
attractiveness, perceptions of 52
Ausubel, David 102
authentic caring 130, 134, 149, 157, 183

behaviors: helping 164; high-risk 20; prosocial 152, 164, 165
Benson, Peter 21
Bernadowski, C. 82
Best, K. M. 112
Bishop, Penny 3, 186, 188
Blake, J. 50
body mass index (BMI) 52
bonding to school **15**, 16
brain: growth during adolescence 69–71, 179–180; reward pathways in 120
Branje, S. 165
Brown, Chris 201
Broyhill, Amie 157, 158, 161
Buchanan, R. 155

Canfield, J. 154, 169
caring **15**; authentic 130, 134, 149, 157, 183; neighborhood **14**; school climate **14**

Carlo, G. 165
C'de Baca, J. 135
Central Cabarrus High School 198
characteristic behavioral changes during puberty 43
childhood 50
children 42; connections with peoples and pets 68; cope with traumatic experiences 112; learn to interpret sensory information 111; things about themselves 115
Clapp, Amanda 89–94
classrooms 2, 5, 183; communities 28, 38, 61–62, 196–198; environment 5, 60; exploring personal identities 183; need for physical flexibility in 61
collaboration 38, 61–62, 185
Collaborative for Academic, Social, and Emotional Learning (CASEL) 160
color, adultification of students of 50–51
commitment to learning **15**, 16
community/communities: classroom 28, 38, 61–62, 196–198; learning 195–196; religious **15**; values youth **14**
competence/competency 158–159; academic 153–157, 185; cultural **15**; social 150–153, 159–161, 185
concept maps 102–104
conflict resolution **15**, 17
connections/connectedness: among brain cells 69; among students' thoughts and actions 155–157; between emotions, attention, and memory 71; helping teachers plan lessons 94; school 152, 169, 181, 187; sense of 10; thoughts and feelings 68–69, 94–101
creativity **14**, 72, 78
critical thinking 72, 81, 123
Crocetti, E. 165
Crone, E. 78, 118, 152
Csikszentmihalyi, M. 95–96
cultural competence **15**
cultural images, examining 170–171
cultural socialization 125

Davis, K. 119
DECIDE model 77–78
decision-making **15**, 70, 76, 78, 179

deep learning 81, 84–85, **84**
Developmental Assets framework 12–13, 151, 186; External Assets 13, **14–15**, 17; Internal Assets 13, **15**, 16–17, 26; ratings of assets 17; research continuation 18
developmental changes: intellectual and emotional development patterns 179–180; personal identity development 180–181; physical and sexual development patterns 178–179; social and moral development patterns 181–183; understanding and supporting 177–178
developmental relationships 20, 21
Doherty, J. 155

education: importance to identify nutritional issues 54; parental 179
Educational Psychology: A Cognitive View (Ausubel) 102–103
educators 177, 179
emotional/emotions 68, 71; awareness 95; development 94, 180; learning 95, 97; shaping attention 68; on thinking and learning 71–72
emotional maturation 95
empathy 162, 164, 165–168, 182
empowerment **14**
energy level and appetite of adolescents, fluctuations in 51–52; changes in nutrition 52–56; changes in sleep patterns 56–57
Epstein, R. 50
equality **15**
Erikson, E. 114
essential skills for adolescents 163, 169
ethnic-racial identity (ERI) 123–130, 133, 181
ethnic-racial socialization 125–126
evidence-based practices 4
executive functions of adolescents 70, 179
exploratory and risk-taking abilities of adolescence 70
External Assets 13, **14–15**, 17
Eyer, Ashley 198

family/families: boundaries **14**; experiences 125; listening to children 42; support **14**
Faye, A. 112, *113*

feelings 68; connecting with thoughts 68–69, 94–101; of discomfort during adolescence 179
Figurative Transformation activity 121–123
Flow Theory 95–96; case study 97–101; flow experiences 96–97
fMRI 69
friendships, formation of 153, 181

Gardner, H. 119
Garmezy, N. 112
gender identity 123–130, 133
Goddard, R. D. 21
González, T. 50

Hansen, K. 155
Hargett, Jaleisha 47–50, 123–124
Harrison, Lisa 3, 186, 188
helping behaviors 164
high-risk behaviors 20
high school classrooms 42
homework **15**, 16
honesty **15**
hormonal changes during puberty 44–45
Hoy, W. K. 21
Huang, C. Y. 124–125
hypothalamic-pituitary-adrenal axis (HPA axis) 45
hypothalamic-pituitary-gonadal axis (HPG axis) 45

"I am poem" by Faye A. 112, *113*
identity 180; definition 171–172; exploration 114–115; perceptions of 180
identity development of adolescents 134, 150; dimensions of positive 111–112; general processes of 129; as negotiated process 118–121; patterns of 114–117
imaginary audience, sense of 118
Immordino-Yang, M. H. 71
information, sense of 150
In Real Life after School Program (IRL) 29–30
instructional experiences 84–88
integrity **15**
intellectual and emotional development of adolescents 179–180; abstract reasoning 78–81; activities for understanding students 102–105; brain growth during adolescence 69–71; connecting thoughts and feelings 68–69, 94–101; creativity 72, 78; expanding powers of reasoning in lessons 81–94; learning to think and feel 71–72; rewards and risks, responses to 72–78; *see also* personal development of adolescents; physical and sexual development of adolescents; social and moral development of adolescents
intelligence 154–155
intentional listening 29
Internal Assets 13, **15**, 16–17, 26
interpersonal competence **15**
intersectional identities 117
introspection 118

Jiang, J. 120
Jones, Jeanneine 1–2, 54, 74, 109

Koot, H. M. 165

learning: challenges during student's developmental stage 5; children's developmental changes 42; commitment to **15**, 16; community 195–196; content area mini-lessons 32–33; emotions on 71–72; experiences in school 134–134; about peer influences 151; about students 200; to think and feel 71–72; to trust teacher 22
learning preferences: content area mini-lessons focus on 32–33; surveys of 30–31
Learning Preferences Self-Assessment Questionnaire 33
LGBTQ identity 129–130, 131–133
life experiences 112, 124, 153, 164, 185
Lincoln, Abraham 83
Lipka, R. 9
listening, intentional 29–30
Listening to Our Teens project 29, 30

marginalization 187, 189
Masten, A. S. 112
Matthews, P. 135
maturation 179; emotional 95; of HPA axis 45; pubertal 46–47, 50, 179
Me Bags activity 134–135

metacognition 71, 80, 82–83, 95, 101, 180
Meyer, A. 155
Middle Grades Curriculum: Voices and Visions of the Self-Enhancing School (Roney and Lipka) 9
Miller, W. R. 135
mindsets 154, 181–182; academic 182; change in 8; fixed 154–156; growth 155, 156, 160, 184; negative 157, 182
MRI 69

National Academies of Sciences, Engineering, and Medicine 18, 44, 45, 46
negative stereotyping during puberty 43
neighborhood boundaries 14
neural pruning 69, 179
neuroplasticity 69, 179, 180
North Stanly High School 201
nucleus accumbens 120
nutrition, changes in 51, 52–56

obesity 52–53
ownership, sense of 182

Paluck, E. L. 150
parents' involvement in schooling 14
peer association 151–152, 169
peer dynamics 126, 150, 181
peer influence 151
peer norms in school settings 126
peer relationships 126–127
personal development of adolescents 111; activities for understanding students 134–136; classroom narrative 131–133; "down memory lane" activity 133; Figurative Transformation activity 121–123; identity development as negotiated process 118–121; learning experiences in school 134–134; negotiating ethnic-racial and gender identity 123–130, 133; patterns of identity development 114–117; resilient sense of self development 111–114; *see also* intellectual and emotional development of adolescents; physical and sexual development of adolescents; social and moral development of adolescents

personal future, positive view of **15**, 112, 114, 182
personal identity development 180–181
personal power **15**, 111, 114, 182
Personal Values Card Sort 135–136, 138–146
perspective-taking 165, 165–168; mature 163–164, *163*; social 163
physical and sexual development of adolescents 38–42, 178–179; activities during 42–43; adultification of students of color 50–51; changes in relationship to physical surroundings 58–61; creating classroom communities 61–62; recognizing fluctuations in energy level and appetite 51–57; understanding changes during puberty 43–50; *see also* intellectual and emotional development of adolescents; personal development of adolescents; social and moral development of adolescents
planning **15**
"poker chip theory" of self-concept 154, 160
positive family communication 14
positive identity **15**, 17
positive peer influence 14
positive relationships 183–184
positive values **15**, 16–17
positive youth development: impacts of exposed to violence 187–188; impacts of poverty and marginalization 187, 189; theory 151; understanding challenges to 186
poverty 187, 189
practice, wisdom of 9
Problem Based Learning (PBL) 172–173
problem-solving 60, 70, 81
Project Based Learning (PBL) 157, 158, 159
Promise of Adolescence, The: Realizing Opportunity for All Youth 18, 23, 45, 46, 70, 72–73, 114
promotive factors for adolescents 112, 114
prosocial behaviors 152, 164, 165
pubertal/puberty 178; changes brain growth during 70; classroom

narrative about 48–50; hormonal changes 44–45; inconsistencies of adolescent thinking during 73–74; maturation 46–47, 50, 179; physical changes 45–46; status 46; tempo 47; timing 47; understanding changes during 43–44; youthful perspectives 44
Purkey, William 199
purpose, sense of **15**, 111, 114, 182
Puvar, D. 151

qualitative research 9–10
Quimby, D. 151

reading: and growing with opportunities 19; for pleasure **15**, 16
reasoning: abstract 78–81; classroom narrative 89–93; deep learning 81, 84–85, **84**; expanding powers in lessons 81; instructional experiences 84–88; metacognition 82–83; SOLO taxonomy 83–84; surface learning 81, 84, **84**; teacher's role in understanding powers of 88–89, 93–94
relationships: changes to physical surroundings 58–61; developmental 21; importance of trust in 21; informal relationships with students 56; positive 183–184; supportive 20–22
Relationships First: Creating Connections that Help Young People Thrive 20, 21
Relationships First Framework elements 183
religious community **15**
research: on adolescent development 11–19; on teaching 9–11
resilience/resiliency 13, 18, 112, 125, 169
resilient sense of self development 111–114, 150, 180, 182, 183, 185
resistance skills **15**
responsibility **15**, 20
responsive teaching practice implementation 184–185
restraint **15**, 16, 17
reward, student's responses to 72–78
Richards, M. 151
risk, student's responses to 72–78
Rivas-Drake, D. 125, 127–128, 130, 134

Roney, K. 9
Rural Southern Voices for Peace (RSVP) 29

safety, physical and emotional 10, **14**, 29, 170
Santiago, C. D. 151
Schon, D. A. 9
school/schooling: bonding to **15**, 16; boundaries **14**; engagement **15**, 16; learning experiences in 134–134; parent involvement in **14**; public perceptions of 4–5
Scott, D. 151
Search Institute 13; Developmental Assets framework 12–18; documenting importance of relationships 21; synthesis on supportive relationships 20
selective attention 70, 179
self-awareness 160, 161–162
self-concept 115
self-definition 124
self development, resilient sense of 111–114
self-efficacy 112
self-esteem **15**, 111, 114, 182
self-regulation 70, 81, 104, 162, 179
self-understandings of adolescents 117
sense-making 181
sensitivity to physical and sexual changes 52
service to others **14**
Shepherd, H. 150
sleep: changes in patterns 51, 56–57; importance of 179
small steps approach 159–161
Social and Emotional Learning (SEL) 160
social and moral development of adolescents 149, 168–169, 181–183; academic competence 153–157; classroom narrative 158–159; expanding perspectives and promoting ethics 161–168; social competence 150–153, 159–161; *see also* intellectual and emotional development of adolescents; personal development of adolescents; physical and sexual development of adolescents
social competence 150, 185; formation of friendships 153; peer association

151; prosocial behavior 152; small steps approach 159–161; *see also* academic competence
social competencies **15**, 186
social justice **15**
social learning 97
social media 47, 52, 119–121
socio-emotional skills 20
stereotypes 170–171
Stevens, A. P. 120–121
Stormshak, E. A. 124–125
Strahan, David 1–2, 9, 67, 109–110, 155
strength-based approach 112, 114
Structure of Observed Learning Outcomes taxonomy (SOLO taxonomy) 83–84
Student Choice and Student Engagement (Travis) 59
students: adultification of color 50–51; with fixed mindsets 155; guidance counselors' support for 56; importance of trust in relationships among 21–22; informal relationships with 56; learning experiences 2; middle school 20; mindsets 154–155, 157; process of observing 177; sense of information 150; sense of self development 115; think about themselves 115
Successful Middle School, The: This We Believe (Bishop and Harrison) 3, 4, 176, 186–190
support/supportive/supporting 13, **14**; adolescents' social well-being 29; classroom climate 26; development of student 183; ethnic-racial identity 130; proactive 117; relationships 20–22
surface learning 81, 84, **84**

teachers 177; case studies with 9–11; conscientious, proactive support to student 117; creating classroom communities 28; facing challenges of policy issues 128–129; guidance counselors' support for 56; identifying student's self development 115–116; importance of trust in relationships among 21–22; and influential adolescents 150–151; learning experiences 2–3; listening to children 42; mailbox 64; role in development of ethnic identity 127–128; role in empowering students 97; role in understanding powers of reasoning 88–89, 93–94; sharing about personal life 64–65; uses of concept maps for 102–104; veteran 3
teaching 1–3, **191**; activities for understanding students 28–32; awareness for improving teaching practice 61–62; classroom communities 185; content area mini-lessons 32–33; creating positive relationships 183–184; essential element of 177; experiences 6–8; framework for 26–28, *27*; Hutchison's story 6–8, 190, 191–202; implementing responsive teaching practices 184–185; realistic goals in 200–202; research on adolescent development 11–19; research on teaching 9–11; with spirit of adventure *190;* supportive relationships 20–22; in synchronization with adolescent development 3–6; understanding and responding to developmental changes 22–26, 177–183; understanding challenges to positive youth development 186–190; understanding dynamics of 8–9
temporal discrepancy 70–71
think-aloud activities 104–105
thinking/thoughts 68; changes in 72; connecting with feelings 68–69, 94–101; development of 69; emotions on 71–72; representational *79*; stop-start processes of 73; students responded to verbal problem **80**, 81
threshold of engagement 27–28, 177, 185
time: constructive use of **14;** at home **15**
Tomlin, Dru 163
transition from childhood to adulthood 70

Travis, Joellyn Marie 59
trust(ing) 38, 61–62, 170, 185; caring teacher 22; importance in relationships 21; questioning to nurture relationships 63–64
Tschannen-Moran, M. 21

Umaña-Taylor, A. J. 125, 127–128, 130, 134

Van der Graaf, J. 165
veteran teachers 3
voluntary responsive inhibition 70, 179

Wang, J. 112
Wells, H. C. 154, 169
White, Madison 1–2, 23–26, 61, 110, 121, 172
Wilbourne, P. 135
Willingham, D. T. 57, 81–82, 88
wisdom of practice 9–10
working memory 70, 83, 89, 179

youth: "App Generation" 119; development 4, 11; programs **14;** as resources **14**

Zhang, D. 112
Zimmerman, M. A. 112

Made in the USA
Coppell, TX
12 September 2024

37248403R10128